Bicycle Stamps

BICYCLE STAMPS

BIKES AND CYCLING ON THE WORLD'S POSTAGE STAMPS

DAN GINDLING

BICYCLE BOOKS

FROM

Motorbooks International
Publishers & Wholesalers

Printed in China

First published in 1997 by Motorbooks International Publishers & Wholesalers, 729 Prospect Avenue, PO Box 1, Osceola, WI 54020-0001 USA

© Dan Gindling, 1997

Motorbooks International is a certified trademark, registered with the United States Patent Office

Motorbooks International books are also available at discounts in bulk quantity for industrial or sales-promotional use. For details write to Special Sales Manager at the Publisher's address

Library of Congress Cataloging-in-Publication Data

Gindling, Dan, 1962–
Bicycle Stamps: Bikes and cycling on the world's postage stamps.
1. Cycling. 2. Bicycles. 3. Philately.
I. Authorship: Gindling, Dan.
II. Title. III. Title: Bicycle Stamps
Bibliography: p.
96-84576

ISBN 0-933201-78-8

Printed in China by Norman Graphics Printing Co., LTD.

For Kimberlee

Acknowledgments

I would like to thank Steve Malone for his invaluable help, and Sheldon Ruckens, a San Diego stamp dealer, who helped expand both my philatelic aptitude and my bicycle stamp collection.

Table of Contents

1. **Bicycles on Stamps** **9**

   Before the Bicycle 9
   Before the Postage Stamp 9
   The First Bicycle Postage Stamp . 10
   History of the Bicycle on Stamps . 10
   Commemorative Stamps 10
   Olympic Stamps 11
   Postal Carriers 11
   Semi-Postals 12
   Other Philatelic Stuff 12
   Make It Your Hobby 13

2. **Bicycle History on Stamps 14**

   The Draisienne 14
   Adding Pedals 15
   The Ordinary 15
   Safety Bikes 16
   The Safety Bicycle 16
   Modern Bicycles 17
   Other Bicycle History Sets 17
   Listing of Stamps 19

3. **Stamps at the Olympics 21**

   The Modern Games 21
   The First Olympic Bike Stamp . . 22
   Other Olympic Bicycle Stamps . . 22
   Olympic Mascots 23
   On the Track 24
   Who's No. 1? 24
   The IOC Centennial 25
   Listing of Stamps 25

4. **Bicycle Racing Stamps . 52**

   First Bicycle Racing Stamp 52
   Popular Races 53
   Track Racing 54
   Eddie Merckx 55
   Triathlon 55
   Listing of Stamps 56

5. **Semi-Postals** **71**

   European Semi-Postals 71
   Asian Semi-Postals 73
   Semi-Postal Overprints 73
   Listing of Stamps 74

6. **Postal Carriers** **80**

   Unusual Postal Bikes 80
   Women Postal Carriers 81
   Boy Scouts 82
   Other Interesting Postal Carrier
      Stamps 82
   Listing of Stamps 83

7. **Special Subjects** **89**

   Art 89
   Transportation 90
   Health and Safety 90
   Animated Characters 91
   Other Subjects 91
   Listing of Stamps 91

8. **Local Issues** **119**

   Coolgardie 119
   Fresno–San Francisco 121
   Cape of Good Hope–Mafeking . 121
   Couriers for Upper Italy 121
   Other Notable Local Issues . . . 122

9. **Booklets** **123**

10. **Other Postal Items** . . **126**

    First Day Covers 126
    Maximum Cards 129
    Postal Stationery 129

11. The Artists 131

Professor Paul Flora, Austria . . . 131
LeRoy Neiman, United States . . 135
Sue Passmore, Australia 136
Gyula Vasarhelyi, England 136

12. Errors on Stamps . . 138

13. Getting Started . . . 139

Pertinent Contacts 140
Glossary 141

Bibliography 142

Index 144

1

Bicycles on Stamps

More than 1,500 stamps and other postal issues with images of cycles or cyclists have been identified. All those known and issued to date are listed in this book, and a good many of them illustrated, divided over chapters each dealing with a particular aspect.

Before the Bicycle

Before the bicycle, people either got around by horse or on foot. A horse required a lot of care and expense, and foot travel took a great deal of time. A magazine of the early bicycle era described the two-wheeled invention as "the animal which costs but little to keep. It does not eat cartloads of hay. It is easy to handle — it never rears up — it won't bite. It needs no check rein or halter, and will lean lovingly against the nearest support."

Before the Postage Stamp

Before the prepaid adhesive postage stamp, the person receiving the mail paid a tax dependent on the distance the letter or parcel had traveled. In 1837 an English school

teacher named Rowland Hill published a pamphlet advocating postal reform. One of the ideas presented was to sell prepaid postage stamps. Hill's reforms were instituted, and the world's first adhesive postage was issued on 6 May 1840.

The First Bicycle Postage Stamp

The marriage of the postage stamp and the bicycle took place 59 years after the postage stamp's debut, and 82 years after the invention of the Draisienne, the first serious adult bike. Cuba, then under U.S. military rule, performed the ceremony on 15 December 1899 by issuing an orange-colored, 10-centavos Special Delivery stamp carrying an illustration of a man riding a one-speed bike. (It's interesting to note that the world's first bicycle stamp contained a misspelling — "Immediata" instead of "Inmediata" — which led to the stamp being reissued three years later with the spelling corrected.)

Since the first bike stamp, over 1,500 bicycle postage stamps, souvenir sheets, and booklets have been produced worldwide, not including the vast number of local issues and cinderellas (see below). And it's been a virtual history course in bicycle design.

History of the Bicycle on Stamps

The first adult bike — the Draisienne, named after its inventor, Baron Karl von Drais of Karlsruhe, Germany — has been commemorated on numerous stamps, as was Pierre Michaux's velocipede — the first mass-produced bike with pedals, and the big-wheeled Ordinary. Illustrations of BMX bikes, tandems, racing bicycles, tricycles, pedal-powered rickshaws, even the newest craze — mountain bikes — can be found on postage stamps.

Commemorative Stamps

Why do countries issue stamps with bicycle images? There's really no one answer. Sometimes a nation wishes to commemorate a cycling event taking place in the country. Like Canada in 1974, when the World Cycling Championships came to Montreal resulting in an 8-cent value "commemorative" stamp being issued. Or Italy, for the 50th running of the Giro d'Italia in 1967. Or Columbia, whose postal service produced a 60-peso stamp in 1986 to commemorate the 25th anniversary of the National Coffee Producers Association's sponsorship of Colombia's National Cycling Team.

Bicycle postage stamps have also been issued by nations to promote awareness of public safety or health. For instance, the Netherlands, where it seems everyone rides a bike, has produced numerous stamps promoting safe bicycle operation.

Bicycles have appeared on stamps commemorating famous military battles, on scouting stamps, stamps celebrating train travel, Christmas stamps, famous paintings; even Russian cosmonauts pedaling stationary bikes, and animals atop two-wheelers have been illustrated on stamps.

Olympic Stamps

The Olympics have been a popular stamp subject. More than 400 bicycle stamps have been produced — more than a quarter of all bike stamps — for 12 Olympic Games, starting with the Helsinki Olympics in 1952. The Olympics have become so popular for stamp-issuing countries that since 1960, the number of stamps produced carrying an illustration of a bike during an Olympic year has been double, sometimes triple the number of bike stamps issued in each of the three preceding non-Olympic years.

Postal Carriers

Another favorite bicycle stamp theme has been postal carriers: the men and women who actually deliver the stamps that so many people collect. In fact, the first U.S. bicycle postage stamp showed an illustration of a postal carrier riding a bicycle. A postal carrier is also the subject of one of the world's most valuable bike stamps, because he's riding the bike upside down. When 200 two-color 1910 Cuban 10-centavos Special Delivery stamps were accidentally

produced with the blue plate printed upside down, the stamp became a rare "invert." While the regular 10-centavos stamp is worth around $11 today, the invert is valued at over $700.

Semi-Postals

In addition to the price of postage, stamps have, at times, carried surcharges to raise money for various organizations and causes within the issuing country. These stamps are called semi-postals. Germany and the Netherlands, as well as a number of other countries, have produced numerous semi-postal stamps showing bicycles.

Other Philatelic Stuff

In addition to postage stamps, philatelic materials (stamp stuff) of interest to the bicycle stamp collector include souvenir sheets, booklets, first day covers, postal stationery, maximum cards, fancy cancels, local issues, and cinderellas.

Souvenir sheets are colorful adhesive sheets usually commemorating an event or anniversary, often containing one or more postage stamps within its borders.

Booklets, first produced by Luxembourg in 1895, include several stamps bound together.

First day covers comprise an envelope with a stamp affixed, possibly carrying an illustration (called a cache), as well.

Postal stationery includes postal cards, envelopes with postal stamps embossed or imprinted, and aerograms.

Maximum cards are postal cards with the stamp affixed to the picture side of the card.

Fancy cancels are cancellation marks that show, in addition to the date and location a piece of mail received postal service, a black and white illustration (of a bicycle or any one of a myriad other topics).

Local issues are stamps used on mail delivered in a limited area by a government agency or private concern.

Cinderellas are stamp-like items that carry no postage value (for example, Easter Seals, a few of which show bicycles).

Make It Your Hobby

The beginning bicycle philatelist (someone who collects stamp stuff) should not feel overwhelmed by the plethora of bicycle stamps and ancillary materials. While some collectors may try to acquire everything, others stick to, say, mint stamps, or first day covers, or local issues. It's all according to your personal taste — and your pocketbook. Chapter 13 shows you in detail how to go about it.

Whether you want to collect it all or just a portion, you can be assured of one thing: a lifelong adventure. Because just as a bicycle wheel turns over and over when ridden, bicycle stamps (and other two-wheeled philatelic materials) keep coming out year after year, and acquiring the philatelic gems is a lot of the fun.

2

Bicycle History on Stamps

"Old bikes" are one of the most frequently used themes for bicycle stamps. Although not always historically correct, these stamps allow the collector to trace the historical development of the bicycle and cycling.

The Draisienne

While most historians consider Baron Karl von Drais of Karlsruhe, Germany, the inventor of the bicycle, many stamp issuing countries seem to disagree on the actual year the Draisienne was invented.

The Republic of Mali, in West Africa, issued a 3-stamp bicycle set in 1968 and placed the year of invention as 1808. Cuba meanwhile, in a 5-stamp "Bicycle Retrospective" set, specified 1813. Czechoslovakia used the year 1820 in a 5-stamp "Historic Bicycles" set. The island of Barbuda set the date of invention of the world's "first steerable bicycle" as 1818. And Germany, the inventor's home country, specified 1817 in a 4-stamp "Bicycling in Germany" semi-postal set, issued in 1985. Most historians today agree with the Germans.

Adding Pedals

But which country identified the next big leap in bicycle design — pedals? And the real inventor of the pedal-driven bicycle? While the French generally hold Pierre and Ernest Michaux of France to be the father-and-son team who first performed the pedal feat, and Americans are becoming more and more aware that it was probably another Frenchman, Pierre Lallement, the British long thought that a Scottish black-smith named Kirkpatrick Macmillan was the real inventor. The design attributed to Macmillan was pictured on a stamp issued by Mongolia in 1982 as part of an 8-stamp "Historic Bicycles" set. It had pedals attached to rods, connecting to crank-arms driving the back wheel. Thus this machine could be propelled without the rider's feet touching the ground.

Interestingly, many quasi-historians also believe that it must have been Macmillan who, in 1842, was reportedly convicted of a traffic offense for knocking over a child while pedaling a cycle. They jump to the conclusion that the "gentleman" was Macmillan (no, blacksmiths in those days were not referred to as gentlemen), and that the "cycle" was indeed a two-wheeled contraption (and not the more common tri-cycle or even quadracycle), and that the machine was of indeed his own invention.

The Ordinary

The next leap in bicycle design was the Ordinary, arguably the most awkward looking of bicycles. The Ordinary featured a huge diameter front wheel and a tiny rear wheel. The bicycle could travel faster (the bigger the front wheel, the faster the bike) and cover more ground than any bike before it. More than 20 stamps and souvenir sheets carrying illustrations of the Ordinary have been issued. Some noteworthy issues are Great Britain's release in 1978 of a 4-stamp

set to commemorate the 100th anniversary of the British Cycling Federation and Cyclists Touring Club. In 1985 Austria released a Paul Flora–designed stamp showing carnival riders atop Ordinaries. Flora's illustration is one of the most whimsical of all bicycle stamps.

Safety Bikes

While the Ordinary could get its rider to his/her destination faster and travel farther, it had its drawbacks, mainly its inherent instability. The machine proved hard to mount and dismount, and because the front wheel was steered and driven, at the same time, the design caused tired arms.

The Safety Bicycle

The 1982 Mongolia stamp set pictured "Lawson's Bicyclette," patented in 1879, which was perhaps the first safety bicycles with a chain-drive to the rear wheel. Lawson's invention was also pictured on a stamp in Cuba's Retrospective set. An Ireland 3-stamp set, issued in 1991, illustrated an 1886 "Starley Rover," the real precursor to today's bicycle design. The Rover placed the rider between two wheels of the same diameter, and the bike was driven by a chain attached to the rear wheel — just as today's bikes are.

After the safety bikes, many "bicycle history" stamp sets left an enormous gap between design innovations. The Mongolia set jumped from the 1879 Lawson to a 1980s "Modern Bike," while the Cuban Retrospective set left a similar void. What happened to bicycle design in those hundred-odd years? In 1888, the Scottish veterinarian John Dunlop of Belfast, Ireland, first mounted the pneumatic tire, giving cyclists a more comfortable ride. (Dunlop's contribution to cycling has never been commemorated on a bicycle stamp). The development of the 3-speed hub made pedaling hills easier, and, just before World War II, the invention of the derailleur made 5-speed, and then 10-speed (meanwhile advanced to 16-

speed and even 18-speed), racing bikes, and now 24-speed mountain bikes popular.

Modern Bicycles

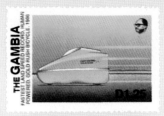

In 1988, Vietnam issued an interesting 7-stamp set of "Modern Bicycles." Included were stamps picturing a children's bike with training wheels, a BMX bike, a Columbia RX5, an English touring bike, and a Rabasa Derbi (which looks similar to an adult folding bicycle). The two most interesting stamps in the set, however, showed a 1960 Bowden Spacelander, and sleek disc-wheeled bike identified as a "Huffy."

The Spacelander was the brainchild of Ben Bowden, a British automobile designer. First constructed of metal, and later of fiberglass, the Spacelander weighed less than 50 pounds, but was reported to have been "too weird looking" for the general public. Whilst in its own time the design never became popular, and less than 600 were produced, they are now sought-after collector's items.

The "Huffy" bike pictured on the 20-dong value stamp was actually a hand-made bike built by Mike Melton for the U.S. cyclists in the 1984 Olympics. Huffy, a manufacturer of mass-produced bikes sold through discount and department stores, sponsored the Olympic cycling effort, and in return received logo placement on the Olympic bikes. Department stores carrying the Huffy brand certainly had none of the sleek, multi-thousand dollar Olympic Huffy bikes for sale at any of their locations.

Other Bicycle History Sets

The 1985 "Bicycling in Germany" set coincided with von Drais' 200th birthday and the United Nations' "International Year of Young People." The set features four early cycles: a Draisienne, an 1886 Ordinary, an 1887 safety bike which included a spring-type shock absorber, and an 1888 adult three-wheeler.

The postal authority of Berlin produced a 4-stamp bicycle set in 1985 as well. The

stamps show a 1868 Bussing bicycle, patterned after a French velocipede; an 1885 child's tricycle; a 1925 Opel racing bike, and a 1925 "J-Rad." Designed by Paul Jaray, a Swiss zeppelin maker, the J-Rad was a recumbent bicycle with foot levers connected to the rear wheel so as to give the bicycle three different gear ratios.

The 1993 Cuba set mentioned earlier included a 3-centavo value stamp picturing a reproduction of a sketch once attributed to Leonardo da Vinci (at first thought to have been drawn by a student of his, but now widely considered a fake inserted in recent times). The illustration shows a contrivance with two wheels of the same diameter, a pedal-crank-chain configuration, a seat, and a steering mechanism (which, as it appeared, wouldn't work).

A year earlier, the African nation of Tanzania produced a 7-stamp set, beginning with an 1813 Russian push-scooter contraption, continuing with three German-designed bikes of the 1800s, then a couple of Italian, aerodynamic bicycles, and finally a Swedish ladies' bike. The souvenir sheet shows the Kangaroo, an early British safety bike that looked like a scaled-down Ordinary with a chain-driven front wheel.

Another bike history set, issued in 1978 by Togo, pictures, on a 50 franc value stamp, an 1870 bicycle patterned after the American Star (which has the small wheel in front and the large wheel in the back) with a side-car attached. The souvenir sheet illustrates a modern couple riding a tandem, their hands in the air as if holding up the two stamps on the sheet.

And while not a set of stamps, but a single issue, Gambia in 1988 produced a postage stamp showing a human powered vehicle, arguably the most radical looking of bicycle designs. The pictured vehicle — the Gold Rush — won a $15,000 prize from the DuPont Corporation in May 1986 as the first HPV to exceed 65 miles per hour. With "Fast" Freddy Markum at the control, pedaling a strip of road near Yosemite National Park in California, the Gold Rush zoomed through a 200-meter timed shoot at 65.484 miles per hour, thereby claiming the prize.

Listing of Stamps

Antigua and Barbuda

1987: First Steerable Bicycle
70 Cent

Barbuda

1987: First Steerable Bicycle
70 Cent
Overprinted "Barbuda Mail" on
Antigua-Barbuda stamp

Bhutan

1988: Transportation Innovations
2 Ngultrum

Congo, Peoples Republic

1969: Bicycles and Motorcycles
50 Franc
75 Franc
80 Franc
85 Franc

Cuba

1993: Bicycle Retrospective
6-stamp set

Czechoslovakia

1979: History of Bicycles
5-stamp set

France

1983: Centenary of Death of Pierre Michaux
1.60 Franc

Gambia

1988: Transportation Innovations
1.25 Dalasy
Human powered vehicle

Great Britain

**1978: Centennial British Cycling Federation
and Cyclists Touring Club**
4-stamp set

Ireland

1991: Irish Cycles
3-stamp set
The above stamps also appear
on a 3-stamp souvenir sheet

Mali

1968: Historic Bicycles and Automobiles
2 Franc
10 Franc
50 Franc

Mongolia

1982: Historic Bicycles
8-stamp set
1-stamp souvenir sheet – 4 Tugrik

Niger

1968: 150th Anniversary of the Bicycle
100 Francs

Poland

1986: Warsaw Cyclists' Society
100th Anniversary
6-stamp set

Tanzania

1992: History of the Bicycle
7-stamp set
1-stamp souvenir sheet – 350 Shilling

Togo

1978: History of the Bicycle
6-stamp set
90 and 100 Franc
These stamps also appear on a
2-stamp souvenir sheet

United States

1982: Transportation
5.9 Cents

1985: Transportation
6 Cents

1988: Transportation
24.1 Cents

Venezuela

1981: History of Transport
1 Bolivar

Vietnam

1989: Modern Bicycles
7-stamp set

3

Stamps at the Olympics

Forget about money and endorsements as if your name is Coroebus of Elis, the first recorded winner at the inaugural Olympic Games, in 776 B.C. Coroebus, a baker by trade, won the only event of the Games: a foot race the length of the stadium in Olympia, Greece, and was awarded a simple olive branch, cut from a sacred tree with a gold-handled knife and fashioned into a wreath. The Greeks believed the branch would give him vitality.

As the Games continued, and events like wrestling and chariot racing were added, the winners' spoils not only included the customary olive crown but the permission to erect a statue of themselves in Olympia, but only after three victories.

The Ancient Games flourished uninterrupted for almost 1,200 years until shut down by Theodosius, emperor of Rome, in 394 A.D. He had labeled the event a pagan ritual.

The Modern Games

Fifteenhundred years later, Frenchman Baron Pierre de Coubertin renewed the Olympics. In 1894 he assembled 79 dele-

gates from 12 countries at the first International Athletics Congress (the precursor to the International Olympic Committee). Two years later his vision of friendly competition to promote relationships between countries became a reality and the modern Olympics were born.

Attracting 311 participants — all men — from 13 nations to Athens, Greece, the first modern Olympic Games saw athletes compete in nine sports, among them bicycle racing (four track races and two road contests, including a 12-hour endurance competition, all won by French cyclists). Each Olympic victor won, not an olive branch, but a silver medal. (It wasn't until the 1908 London Olympic Games before the familiar of gold, silver, and bronze medals were first used as awards for the top three placings in each event.)

Greece didn't take long to issue the first set of Olympic postage stamps, in 1896, to commemorate the return of the Games. The 12-stamp set didn't include a bicycle illustration, but instead commemorated "classic" Olympic events like chariot racing and boxing.

The First Olympic Bike Stamp

A half-century passed after the inaugural modern Olympic Games before an Olympic postage stamp bore the image of a bike. Monaco did the honors, producing a set of 10 Olympic stamps for the 1952 Helsinki Games, issued not during the Olympic year but more than 5 months after the competitions, on February 23, 1953.

Since that day, bicycle stamps have been produced for every Olympic Games: over 400 stamps total — more than a quarter of all bicycle stamps issued to date.

Other Olympic Bicycle Stamps

While most of the Olympic bicycle stamps produced commemorate a country's participation in the Games, some actually immortalize a particular athlete's past performance.

The second Olympic bicycle stamp, produced by the Dominican Republic for the 1956 Melbourne Games, shows Italy's Ercole Baldini, the gold medalist in the road race. This stamp and others in the same set were the first to picture individual winners of Olympic events.

Paraguay seemed to like 1984 1-km champion, Fredy Schmidtke of Germany, so much that they pictured him on two stamps and a souvenir sheet covering two Olympics: the 1984 Los Angeles Games and the 1988 Seoul Games. Not bad for someone whose event required a little over 1 minute of actual Olympic competition.

Other countries have issued an Olympic bicycling stamp and then re-issued it after the Games with an "overprint" of the winner, or to promote an upcoming event. Mark Gorski, of the United States, had his name and the date he won his Olympic gold medal at the 1984 Los Angeles Games overprinted onto a 500 franc stamp produced by the Republic of Cameroon. The first stamp, without the overprint, was issued on 30 April 1984, and the overprinted variety on 10 October.

Unn-al-Qiwain (one of six Persian Gulf sheikdoms that have since formed the United Arab Emirates) went one step further for the 1972 Olympics: they not only printed the winner's name, event, and country, but also a photo of the victorious cyclist inside one of the Olympic rings, left blank when the stamp was first issued.

In 1976, Aitutaki, one of the larger Cook Islands in the South Pacific, produced an Olympic bicycle stamp for the Montreal Olympics, and then reissued the same stamp overprinted commemorating the July 1976 visit of the Queen of England. More than likely the country didn't have time to design and produce a stamp just for the visit, so they reprinted the existing stamp carrying the additional commemorative information.

Olympic Mascots

While Olympic mascots have been around since Munich officials unveiled Waldi the

Dachshund for the 1972 Games, only two mascots — 1984's Sam the Eagle, and 1988's Hodori the Tiger Cub — have appeared on Olympic bicycle stamps or souvenir sheets. And of these, only Hodori has graced an actual bicycle postage stamp, a 30 sucres denomination Ecuador release. Hodori also appeared in the selvedge of a 200 sucres Ecuador souvenir sheet, the selvedge of a South Korea souvenir sheet, and as a part of the border on a full sheet of 1988 Olympic stamps issued by Pakistan. Sam the Eagle made only one bicycle stamp appearance, in the selvedge of a 1984 Olympic souvenir sheet issued by the African nation of Chad.

On the Track

Olympic velodromes have been illustrated on numerous stamps and souvenir sheets, the most popular being Montreal's indoor velodrome built for the 1976 Games. (The velodrome has since been converted into a Bio-Dome.) The Montreal velodrome has appeared on more stamps than any other Olympic velodrome because of its close proximity to Montreal's Olympic Stadium, where the opening and closing ceremonies, and track and field events took place.

Nicaragua produced an interesting Olympic track bicycle souvenir sheet for Olymphilex '85, an annual international Olympic stamp exhibition. The sheet shows a close-up of four track cyclists racing elbow-to-elbow. The art used for the sheet was gleaned from a photo of the victorious 1984 Australian Olympic Pursuit Team. However, the Nicaragua sheet shows the four cyclists, all on track bikes, but they appear to be racing on the streets, not in a velodrome. And the artist has changed the colors of the jerseys so the riders appear to be not competing for Australia, but four different nations.

Who's No. 1?

The United States, whose cyclists have competed in every modern Olympic Game except the 1980 Moscow Olympics, has issued Olympic bicycle stamps only for the 1972, 1984, and 1996 Olympics. The country that has produced bicycle stamps for the most Olympic Games is Mongolia, with eight Olympics beginning with the 1964 Tokyo Games, followed by Poland with seven, and Costa Rica and Guinea with five each.

The IOC Centennial

In 1994, numerous countries released postage stamps commemorating the 100th anniversary of the formation of the International Olympic Committee, and to honor the founder of the modern Olympic movement, Baron Pierre de Coubertin. A handful of these stamps carried a bicycle illustration.

Listing of Stamps

Afars and Issas

1976 Olympics
15 Fils

Aitutaki

1976 Olympics
15 Cents
Stamp also appears on 4-stamp souvenir sheet
Also issued with "Royal Visit, July 1976" overprint
Overprint also appears on 4-stamp souvenir sheet

Ajman

1968 Olympics
2 Riyals

1968 Olympics
5 Riyals
Cycling medal

1969: 1968 Olympic Winners
1-stamp souvenir sheet – 10 Riyals

1969: 1968 Olympic Winners
1 Dirham
Bicycle symbol only
Also appears on 1-stamp souvenir sheet

2 Dirhams
Also appears on 1-stamp souvenir sheet

10 Dirhams
Bicycle symbol only
Also appears on 1-stamp souvenir sheet
Also issued with "Munich-Germany" overprint
Overprint also appears on 1 stamp souvenir sheet

5 Riyals

Bicycle symbol only
Also appears on 1-stamp souvenir sheet
Also issued with "Munich-Germany" overprint
Overprint also appears on 1 stamp souvenir sheet

10 Riyals
Bicycle symbol only
Also appears on 1-stamp souvenir sheet

10 Riyals
Bicycle symbol only
Also appears on 1-stamp souvenir sheet
Also issued with "Munich-Germany" overprint
Overprint also appears on 1 stamp souvenir sheet

1-stamp souvenir sheet – 15 Riyals
Bicycle symbol in selvedge

1969: 1968 Olympic Winter Games
1-stamp souvenir sheet – 5 Riyals
No bicycle depicted on stamp
"Gold Medal to Pierre Trentin Cycle Race..."
imprinted on border

1971: 1972 Olympics
1 Riyal
Also appears on 1-stamp souvenir sheet

1971: 1972 Olympics
20 Dirhams
Also appears on 1-stamp souvenir sheet

1972: Olympics Winners – D. Morelon
5 Riyals
Stamp issued in 3 varieties

Albania

1963: 1964 Olympics
6 Lek

1964 Olympic Games
3 Lek

1968 Olympics
1-stamp souvenir sheet – 2 Lek
Velodrome

1972 Olympics
20 Quintar

1975: 1976 Olympics
5 Quintar

1-stamp souvenir sheet – 2.15 Lek
Bicycle symbol only

Algeria

1972 Olympics
25 Centimes

Andorra, French

1996 Olympics
3 Francs

Angola

1992 Olympics
180 Kwanza

Antigua

1976 Olympics
1 Dollar
Also appears on 4-stamp souvenir sheet

Antigua and Barbuda

1984 Olympics
3 Dollars

1995: 100th Anniversary of International Olympic Committee
6 Dollars

1996 Olympics
1.20 Dollar

Argentina

1984 Olympics
10 Peso

Armenia

1996 Olympics
40 Luma

Aruba

1996 Olympics
130 Cents

Australia

1976 Olympics
40 Cents

1992 Olympics
45 Cents

Bahamas

1972 Olympics
11 Cents
Also appears on 4-stamp souvenir sheet

1976 Olympics
8 Cents
Also appears on 4-stamp souvenir sheet

1988 Olympics
1 Dollar
Also appears on 4-stamp souvenir sheet

1994: Centenary of International Olympic Committee
55 Cents
Stamp on stamp

Bahrain

1992 Olympics
200 Fils

Bangladesh

1984 Olympics
1 Taka

Barbados

1984 Olympics
1 Dollar
Also appears on 4-stamp souvenir sheet

1988 Olympics
25 Cents
Also appears on 4-stamp souvenir sheet

Barbuda

1976 Olympics
1 Dollar
Overprinted "Barbuda" on Antigua stamp
Also appears on 4-stamp souvenir sheet

1984 Olympics
3 Dollars
Overprinted "Barbuda Mail" on
Antigua-Barbuda stamp

Belize

1976 Olympics
35 Cents

1979: 1980 Olympics
5 Dollars
Also appears on 1-stamp souvenir sheet with
stamp revalued at 15 Dollars

1981: History of Olympic Games
1 Dollar

1984 Olympics
2 Dollars

Benin

1976 Olympics
200 Francs
Runner with velodrome in background

1979: 1980 Olympics
10 Francs
Bicycle symbol only

1980 Olympics
200 Francs
Bicycle symbol only
Also issued revalued with "15 Franc" overprint

300 Francs
Bicycle symbol shown on awards platform
Also issued with "Colis Postaux" overprint

Bermuda

1996 Olympics
30 Cents

Brazil

1980 Olympics
4 Cruzado

1992 Olympics
300 Cruzado
Small bicycle

Bulgaria

1976 Olympics
4-stamp souvenir sheet
Bicycle symbol in selvedge

1980 Olympics
35 Stotinki
Also appears on 6-stamp souvenir sheet

1990: 1992 Olympics
42 Stotinki

Burkino Faso

1995: 1996 Olympics
600 Francs
650 Francs

Burundi

1972 Olympics
14 Francs

Caicos Islands

1984 Olympics
65 Cents

Cambodia

1968 Olympics
3 Riel
Also issued in sheetlet of 4

1995: 1996 Olympics
1000 Riel

Cameroun

1984 Olympics
500 Francs
Also issued with "Gorski U.S.A. 03-08-84"
overprint

Canada

1974: 1976 Olympics
8 Cents

1976 Olympics
2 Dollars
Olympic velodrome next to Olympic stadium
Also issued in sheetlets of 8

1992 Olympics
42 Cents

Cayman Islands

1988 Olympics
10 Cents

1992 Olympics
15 Cents
40 Cents
60 Cents
1 Dollar

Central Africa

1979: 1980 Olympics
50 Francs
Also appears on 1-stamp and 6-stamp
souvenir sheets

1-stamp souvenir sheet – 1500 Francs
Bicycle in selvedge

1982: 1984 Olympics
1-stamp souvenir sheet – 1500 Franc
Bicycle symbol in selvedge

1983: 1984 Olympics
200 Francs
Also appears on 1-stamp souvenir sheet

1987: 1992 Olympics
265 Francs
Also appears on 1-stamp and 5-stamp
souvenir sheets

1990: 1992 Olympics
1-stamp souvenir sheet – 1000 Francs
Bicycle in selvedge

1993: 100th Anniversary of the
International Olympic Committee
100 Francs
Also appears on 9-stamp souvenir sheet

1996 Olympics
350 Francs
600 Francs

Chad

1969: 1968 Olympic Winners
1 Franc – Trentin
1 Franc – Morelon & Trentin
1 Franc – Vianelli
1 Franc – Rebillard
All above stamps also issued with "Munich
1972" overprint

1972 Olympics
1-stamp souvenir sheet – 300 Francs

1972 Olympics
1-stamp souvenir sheet – 250 Francs
Bicycle in selvedge

1972 Olympics
1-stamp souvenir sheet – 250 Francs

1982: 1984 Olympics
30 Francs
Also appears on 1-stamp souvenir sheet

1-stamp souvenir sheet – 500 Francs
Bicycle in selvedge

1982: 1984 Olympics
1-stamp souvenir sheet – 1500 Francs
Bicycle in selvedge

1983: 1984 Olympics
1-stamp souvenir sheet – 1500 Francs
Sam the Eagle riding bicycle in selvedge

Chile

1988 Olympics
100 Peso
Also appears on 2-stamp souvenir sheet

China, Republic of (Taiwan)

1964 Olympics
80 Cents

1996 Olympics
5 Yuan

Comoro Islands

1979: 1980 Olympics
25 Francs – Velodrome
50 Francs – Velodrome

1988: 1992 Olympics
125 Francs
Also appears on 4 souvenir sheets: one 1-stamp,
two 3-stamp, one 4-stamp

Congo, Peoples Republic

1975: 1976 Olympics
85 Francs

1992 Olympics
1-stamp souvenir sheet – 750 Francs
Bicycle in selvedge

1993: 1996 Olympics
75 Francs
Also appears on 2 souvenir sheets: 1-stamp,
6-stamp

Cook Islands

1968 Olympics
30 Cents

1992 Olympics
2.25 Dollar

1-stamp souvenir sheet – 6.40 Dollar
Bicycle in selvedge

Costa Rica

1960 Olympics
3 Centavos

1965: 1964 Olympics
10 Centavos

1969: 1968 Olympics
65 Centavos

1980 Olympics
3 Colon

1984 Olympics
11 Colon

Cuba

1991: 1992 Olympics
40 Centavos

1992: OLYMPHILEX '92
40 Centavos

Cyprus

1976 Olympics
60 Milliemes
Bicycle symbol only

Czechoslovakia

1964 Olympics
60 Haleru
Also appears on 10-stamp sheet

1972 Olympics
50 Haleru

1984 Olympics
2 Koruna
Also appears on 4-stamp souvenir sheet

1986: 90th Anniversary International Olympic Committee
2 Koruna

Dahomey

1964 Olympics
85 Francs

Dhufar

1972 Olympics
1 r
Also appears on 8-stamp sheetlet
Also issued with "Scouts Day 1973" overprint
Also issued with "World Cup Munich 1974" overprint
Overprints each appear on 8-stamp sheetlets

1976 Olympics
10 b
Also appears on 8-stamp sheetlet

1980 Olympics
20 b
Also appears on 4-stamp souvenir sheet

Djibouti

1983: 1984 Olympics
2-stamp Souvenir sheet
Bicycle in selvedge

Dominica

1995: 1996 Olympics
2 Dollars

Dominican Republic

1957: 1956 Olympics
7 Centavos
Also appears on 5-stamp sheetlet
Also issued with 4 different overprints:
two "+2" and two "+5"
Overprints each appear on 5-stamp sheetlets

Ecuador

1988 Olympics
30 Sucre

1989: 1988 Olympics
1-stamp souvenir sheet – 200 Sucre
Hodori the Tiger on bike in selvedge

Equatorial Guinea

1972 Olympics
50 Peseta
Souvenir sheets listed with Semi-Postals

1972 Olympics
7-stamp set
Bicycle symbol only on each stamp

1975: 1976 Olympics
35 Ekuele
Bicycle symbol only

1991: 1992 Olympics
250 Francs
Estonia

1996 Olympics
3-stamp souvenir sheet

Ethiopia

1968 Olympics
50 Cents

1972 Olympics
50 Cents

1976 Olympics
90 Cents

1980 Olympics
70 Cents

1996 Olympics
40 Cents

Fujeira

1968 Olympics
25 dh
Also issued in embossed gold
Also issued with "Cycling Road Race ..."
overprint
Also issued with "Munich Germany ..." overprint

1971: 1972 Olympics
3 r

1971: 1972 Olympics
26 dh
Also appears on 30-stamp sheet

1972 Olympics
5 r
Also appears on 1-stamp souvenir sheet
Also issued with "Daniel Morelon" overprint
Overprint also appears on 1-stamp souvenir sheet

Gabon

1968 Olympics
30 Francs
Also appears on 4-stamp souvenir sheet

1972 Olympics
40 Francs over 30 Francs
No bicycle on stamp, "Morelon" overprint

1980 Olympics
3-stamp souvenir sheet
Bicycle in selvedge
Souvenir sheet also issued with overprint
of winners

1992 Olympics
100 Francs

Gambia

1995: 1996 Olympics
3 Dalasy
Also appears on 8-stamp souvenir sheet

German Democratic Republic

1964 Olympics
5 Pfennig
10 Pfennig

1976 Olympics
5 Pfennig
1-stamp souvenir sheet – 5 Mark
Velodrome

1980 Olympics
50 Pfennig

Ghana

1995: 1996 Olympics
300 New Cedi
Velodrome track
Both stamps also appear on 12-stamp
souvenir sheet

Greece

1976 Olympics
11 Drachma
Velodrome

Grenada

1976 Olympics
1 Cent
1-stamp souvenir sheet – 3 Dollars
BIcycle in selvedge

1980 Olympics
40 Cents

1990: 1992 Olympics
4 Dollars

1992 Olympics
50 Cents

Grenada Grenadines

1976 Olympics
½ Cent

1996: Olympic Winners
75 Cents

Guinea

1964 Olympics
200 Francs
1963 Sports stamps overprinted "Jeux Olympique Tokyo 1964" in both orange and carmine

1969: 1968 Olympics
75 Francs

1972 Olympics
200 Francs

1976 Olympics
8.50 Syli

1993: 1996 Olympics
250 Francs
Also appears on 1-stamp and 4-stamp souvenir sheets
1-stamp souvenir sheet – 500 Francs
Bicycle in selvedge

Guinea Bissau

1976 Olympics
3 Peso
Velodrome in background
Also appears on 1-stamp souvenir sheet
1-stamp souvenir sheet – 50 pounds

1984 Olympics
40 Peso
Commemorates both 1932 and 1984
Los Angeles Olympics

Guyana

1988 Olympics
10 Cents
No bicycle on stamp, overprinted in silver
"Women's Cycling Knol"
Also issued with overprint in gold
Both stamps also appear each on 25-stamp sheets

1991: 1992 Olympics
9-stamp souvenir sheet
Montreal velodrome

1993: 1996 Olympics
600 Dollars
Both gold and silver stamps issued
Each stamp appears on 1-stamp, 2-stamp, and
3-stamp souvenir sheets
1-stamp souvenir sheets (both gold and silver)
also issued with "Tour de France 1993" overprint

1995: 1996 Olympics
60 Dollars
Also appears on 8-stamp sheet

Haiti

1972 Olympics
50 Centimes
Picture of Morelon (sprint winner)

1978: 1976 Olympics
25 Centimes

Hong Kong

1992 Olympic Games
2.30 Dollars
Also appears on 4-stamp souvenir sheet
Souvenir sheet also issued with special imprint
for commemoration of opening of Olympics

Hungary

1976 Olympics
7-stamp set
Bicycle symbol only

1992 Olympics
9 Forint

Indonesia

1992 Olympics
300 Rupiah
Bicycle symbol only

Ireland

1988 Olympics
28 Pence
Also appears on 10-stamp souvenir sheet

Isle of Man

**1994: Centenary International Olympic
Committee**
10 Pence

Italy

1960 Olympics
25 Lira – Velodrome

Ivory Coast

1979: 1980 Olympics
150 Francs

Jamaica

1984 Olympics
25 Cents
Also appears on 4-stamp souvenir sheet

1988 Olympics
45 Cents
Also appears on 4-stamp souvenir sheet

Jordan

1964 Olympics
35 Fils

Kazakstan

1996 Olympics
4 Tenge

Korea, North

1964 Olympics
5 Chun

1976: Olympics Winner
25 Chun – Johansson
Also appears on 7-stamp sheet

1976 Olympics
15 Chun – no bicycle on stamp
"France Cycling Sprint Daniel Morelon"
printed on stamp

1976 Olympics
10 Chun
Montreal velodrome

1977: 1976 Olympic Winners
5 Chun – Johansson
3-D stamp

1-stamp souvenir sheet – 60 Chun
No bicycle on stamp, "Johansson, Bernt,
Sweden, cycle..." stamped in gold
3-D stamp

1978: 1980 Olympics
7-stamp souvenir sheet
Bicycle in selvedge

1978: Olympic History Winners
20 Chun
Also appears on 16-stamp souvenir sheet

1979: 1980 Olympics
15 Chun
Also appears on 8-stamp souvenir sheet

1980 Olympics
20 Chun
Also appears on 8-stamp souvenir sheet

1-stamp souvenir sheet – 70 Chun
Bicycle symbols in selvedge

1983: 1984 Olympics
30 Chun
Also appears on 6-stamp sheet and
six 1-stamp souvenir sheets
Bicycle symbol in selvedge

Korea, South

1968 Olympics
7 Won
Bottom line of text flush right

7 Won
Bottom line of text flush left
Above 2 stamps also appear on 2-stamp
souvenir sheet

7 Won
Bicycle symbol only
Bottom line of text flush right

7 Won
Bicycle symbol only
Bottom line of text flush left
Above 2 stamps also appear on 2-stamp
souvenir sheet

Laos

1989: 1992 Olympics
20 Kip

1990: 1992 Olympics
50 Kip

1996 Olympics
30 Kip

Latvia

1996 Olympics
8 Santims

Liberia

1971: 1972 Olympics
3 Cents

1972 Olympics
12 Cents

Libya

1964 Olympics
10 Milliemes
Also appears on 6-stamp souvenir sheet –
all 15 Milliemes

1976 Olympics
1-stamp souvenir sheet – 150 Dirhams

1976 Olympics
15 Dirhams

1983: 1984 Olympics
1-stamp souvenir sheet – 100 Dirhams
bicycle in selvedge

1988 Olympics
150 Dirhams
Also appears 0n 3 sheets: 1-stamp,
2-stamp, 6-stamp

Liechtenstein

1988 Olympics
50 Rappen

1992 Olympics
70 Rappen

1996 Olympics
1.20 Francs

Luxembourg

1968 Olympics
2 Francs

Madagascar

1994: 1996 Olympics
1-stamp souvenir sheet – 1000 Francs
Bicycle in selvedge

Mahra State

1968 Olympics Winners
25 Fils – Pavesi, Italy
Also issued with "Gold Medal 1968 Nordic Ski
Franco Nones" overprint

100 Fils – Rousseau, France
Also issued with "Winner Grenoble 1968
Marielle Goitshel" overprint

Malagasy

1987: 1992 Olympics
1-stamp souvenir sheet – 600 Francs
Bicycle in selvedge

1989: 1992 Olympics
1500 Francs
Also appears on 3 souvenir sheets: 1-stamp,
3-stamp, 6-stamp

1992 Olympics
140 Francs

Malawi

1984 Olympics
30 Tambalas
Also appears on 4-stamp souvenir sheet

Maldive Islands

1960 Olympics
2 Larees
3 Larees
5 Larees
10 Larees
15 Larees

1968 Olympics
1 Rafiyaa
Also issued with "Gold Medal Winners …"
overprint

1972 Olympics
5 Larees

Manama

1968 Olympics
2 Riyal

1968 Olympics
5 Riyal
Also appears on 2-stamp sheet with stamp revalued at 20 Riyal

1969: 1968 Olympic Winners
1-stamp souvenir sheet – 10 Riyal
Morelon and Trentin

1969: 1968 Olympic Winners
1 Dirhams
Hines, athletics
Bicycle symbol only
Also appears on 1-stamp souvenir sheet

2 Dirhams
Trentin, cycling
Also appears on 1-stamp souvenir sheet

10 Dirhams
Neckermann, equestrian
Bicycle symbol only
Also appears on 1-stamp souvenir sheet
Also issued with "Munich–Germany" overprint
Overprint also appears on 1-stamp souvenir sheet

5 Riyals
Klimke, equestrian
Bicycle symbol only
Also appears on 1-stamp souvenir sheet
Also issued with "Munich–Germany" overprint
Overprint also appears on 1-stamp souvenir sheet

10 Riyals
Di Basi, swimming
Bicycle symbol only
Also appears on 1-stamp souvenir sheet

10 Riyals
Linsenhoff, equestrian
bicycle symbol only
Also issued with "Munich-Germany" overprint
Overprint also appears on 1-stamp souvenir sheet
1-stamp souvenir sheet

15 Riyals
U.S.A. basketball team
Bicycle symbol only

Mexico

1967: 1968 Olympics
80 Centavos
Also appears on 2-stamp sheet

1968 Olympics
5 Pesos
Also appears on 2-stamp sheet

Monaco

1953: 1952 Olympics
5 Francs

1988 Olympics
7 Francs
Also appears on 4-stamp souvenir sheet

1993: 101st International Olympic Committee
2.80 Francs

Mongolia

1964 Olympics
60 Mung

1968 Olympics
15 Mung

1976 Olympic Winners
40 Mung
Mitsuo Tsukahara (gymnast)
Velodrome

60 Mung
Gregor Braun, Germany

1980 Olympics
1.20 Tugrik

1984 Olympics
30 Mung

1988 Olympics
60 Mung

1988 Olympics
1-stamp souvenir sheet – 4 Tungrik
Bicycle symbol in selvedge

1989: 1988 Olympic Winners
60 Mung
Gintautas Umaras, USSR

1992 Olympics
30 Mung
1-stamp souvenir sheet – 80 Mung
Bicycle symbol in selvedge

1996 Olympics
1-stamp souvenir sheet – 500 Tugrik
Bicycle symbol in selvedge

1-stamp souvenir sheet – 600 Tugrik
Bicycle symbol in selvedge

Montserrat

1996 Olympics
1.15 Dollar

Morocco

1960 Olympics
15 Francs

1968 Olympics
25 Centimes

1972 Olympics
1 Dirham

1976 Olympics
40 Centimes

1984 Olympics
2 Dirhams
Bicycle symbol only

Mozambique

1980 Olympics
10 Escudo

1988 Olympics
400 Metical

Namibia

1996 Olympics
90 Cents

Netherlands

1972 Olympics
45 Cents

1993: European Youth Olympic Days
70 Cents
80 Cents

Nevis

1992 Olympics
20 Cents

New Zealand

1992 Olympics
45 Cents
Also appears on 4-stamp souvenir sheet
Souvenir sheet also issued with "Columbian
Expo" overprint

1996 Olympics
80 Cents
Also appears on 5-stamp sheet

Nicaragua

1964 Olympics
15 Centavos

1983: 1984 Olympics
6 Cordoba

1985: OLYMPHILEX '85
1-stamp souvenir sheet – 15 Cordoba

1990: 1992 Olympics
30,000 Cordoba

Niger

1976 Olympics
80 Francs
Also appears on two 1-stamp sheets

1-stamp souvenir sheet – 150 Francs
Velodrome in selvedge

1990: 1992 Olympics
1-stamp souvenir sheet – 600 Francs

Nigeria

1984 Olympics
45 Kobo

Niue

1992 Olympics
1-stamp souvenir sheet
Water polo
Bicycle in selvedge

Oman

1994: 100th Anniversary International Olympic Committee
100 Baizas
Bicycle symbol only

Pakistan

1988 Olympics
10 Rupee
Also appears on 10-stamp sheet, also Hodori the Tiger riding a bicycle on
sheet tab

Panama

1960 Olympics
10 Centavos

1964 Olympics
4 Centavos

1968 Olympics
1-stamp souvenir sheet – 70 Centavos

Paraguay

1969: 1968 Olympics Winner
15 Centimos
Also appears on 3-stamp souvenir sheet

1970: 1972 Olympics
15 Centimos

1985: 1984 Olympics
1 Guarani
Also issued with "Barcelona '92 Sede de Las Olimpicas…" overprint

1987: 1988 Olympics
4 Guarani
Also issued with "OLYMPHILEX '88 …" overprint

1987: 1988 Olympics
1-stamp "A" souvenir sheet – 100 Guarani
1-stamp "B" souvenir sheet (same design) – 100 Guarani

Penrhyn

1996 Olympic
5 Shillings

Philippines

1984 Olympics
8.40 Peso
Also appears on 4-stamp souvenir sheet

1988 Olympics
11 Peso

Poland

1960 Olympics
60 Groszy
Past Olympic winners

1968 Olympics
4 Zloty

1972 Olympics
5 Zloty

1976 Olympics
1 Zloty

1984 Olympics
15 Zloty

1992 Olympics
3000 Zloty

1996 Olympics
1 Zloty

Qatar

1972 Olympics
3 Dirhams
Also appears on 6-stamp souvenir sheet

Qu'aiti State in Hadhramaut

1968 Olympics
25 Fils

Ras Al Khaima

1972 Olympics
3 Riyals
Also appears on two 1-stamp sheets –
white and beige

Rwanda

1972 Olympics
6 Francs

1980 Olympics
50 Centimes

Sahara Occidental

1990: 1992 Olympics
40 Paseta

1992 Olympics
60 Paseta

1996 Olympics
136 Paseta

Saint Thomas & Prince Islands

1980 Olympics
11 Dobra
Montreal velodrome

11 Dobra
Moscow velodrome

11 Dobra
Munich velodrome

All 3 stamps also appear on 4-stamp souvenir sheet

1983: 1984 Olympics
18 Dobra
Also appears on 2-stamp and 8-stamp souvenir sheets

Saint Vincent

1980: Sports for all
60 Cents
Includes Olympic rings

1984 Olympics
3 Cents
Male cyclist facing right

3 Cents
Female cyclist facing left

1988 Olympics
2 Dollars
Also appears on 6-stamp souvenir sheet

1-stamp souvenir sheet – 6 Dollars

1992 Olympics
1.50 Dollars

1996 Olympics
9-stamp sheet

Saint Vincent Grenadines

1988 Olympics
2.50 Dollars
Also appears on 6-stamp souvenir sheet

1996: Olympic History
9-stamp souvenir sheet

Saint Vincent Grenadines – Union Islands

1988 Olympics
4 Dollars
Also appears on 4-stamp sheet

1-stamp souvenir sheet – 5 Dollar

Salvador, El

1984 Olympics
40 Centavos

1989: 1992 Olympics
1-stamp souvenir sheet – 1 Colon
Bicycle in selvedge

San Marino

1960 Olympics
10 Lira
Also appears on 4-stamp souvenir sheet

1964 Olympics
120 Lira

1980 Olympics
70 Lira

Saudi Arabia

1986: 90th Anniversary Olympics
20 Halalas
Bicycle symbol only

100 Halalas
Bicycle symbol only

Senegal

1976 Olympics
100 Francs
Also appears on 1-stamp and 6-stamp
souvenir sheets

1984 Olympics
3-stamp Souvenir sheet
Bicycle symbol only

Sharjah

1968 Olympics
1-stamp souvenir sheet – 60 Naye Paise
No bicycle on stamp
"1968 P. Vianelli, Italy, Road Race ..." overprint

1969: 1968 Olympic Winners
1 Rupee
Photo of Morelon
Also appears on 1-stamp souvenir sheet

1972 Olympics
20 Naye Paise
Also appears on 2 sheets: 1-stamp, 10-stamp

1972 Olympics Winners
5 Rupee
"Norelon" incorrect spelling
Also appears on 1-stamp souvenir sheet
Also issued with "Morelon" spelled correctly
Correctly spelled stamp also appears on 1-stamp
souvenir sheet

Sierra Leone

1987: 1988 Olympics
5 Leone

1989: 1988 Olympics Winners
10 Leone

1990: 1992 Olympics
200 Leone

1992 Olympics
300 Leone

South Africa

1996 Olympics
No denomination – "Standard Postage"

Spain

1968 Olympics
3.50 Peseta

1994: 100th Anniversary International
Olympic Committee
29 Peseta

Also appears on 10-stamp sheet with labels

Surinam

1992 Olympics
150 Cents

1996 Olympics
9.00 Gulden

OLYMPHILEX '96
2-stamp souvenir sheet
Bicycle in selvedge

Sweden

1992 Olympics
5.50 Krona

Syria

1988 Olympics
550 Piaster

Tanzania

1984 Olympics
4-stamp souvenir sheet
Bicycle symbol in selvedge

1985: 1984 Olympics
4-stamp souvenir sheet
Bicycle symbol in selvedge

1988 Olympics
20 Shillings
Also issued with "Men's Match Sprint
Lutz Hesslich DDR" overprint

1990: 1992 Olympics
1-stamp souvenir sheet – 400 Shillings

1992 Olymics
20 Shillings

Togo

1960 Olympics
10 Francs

1973: 1972 Olympic Winners
1500 Francs
Also appears on 1-stamp souvenir sheet

1976 Olympics
1000 Francs
Also issued with "Cyclisme Poursuite
Par ..." overprint

1984 Olympics
90 Francs

1984 Olympics
500 Francs
Also issued with "Rolf Golz ..." overprint

1987: 1988 Olympics
200 Francs

Tonga

1988 Olympics
2 Pa'anga
Also appears on 20-stamp sheet

1992 Olympics
3 Pa'anga
Also appears on 20-stamp sheet

Trinidad and Tobago

1968 Olympics
5 Cents

1984 Olympic Games
4 Dollars
Also appears on 4-stamp souvenir sheet

Tunisia

1960 Olympics
5 Millimes

Turkish Republic of Northern Cyprus

1992 Olympics
1500 Turkish Lira

Turks & Caicos Islands

1988 Olympics
70 Cents

1995: 100th Anniversary International Olympic Committee
20 Cents

1996 Olympics
55 Cents

Tuvalu Niutao

1988 Olympics
1.50 Dollars
Also appears on 6-stamp sheet

Tuvalu Nukufetau

1988 Olympics
2 cents
Also appears on 4-stamp sheet

Tuvalu Nukulaelae

1988 Olympics
25 cents
Also appears on 8-stamp sheet

Uganda

1987: 1988 Olympics
50 Shillings

1992 Olympics
500 Shillings

1995: 1996 Olympics
450 Shillings

Ukraine

1992 Olympics
4 Kopecks

Umm Al Qiwain

1972 Olympics Winners
5 Riyals
Also issued with "K. Knudsen..."
overprinted and with picture of rider
Also issued with right portion of stamp trimmed
Also appears on 30-stamp sheet

1973: 1972 Olympics
1 Riyals
Also appears on 16-stamp sheet
Also appears on heavy, ungummed paper, and
16-stamp heavy paper sheet

1 Riyals – larger stamp
Also appears on three 1-stamp souvenir sheets:
rose, blue, and white borders
Also appears on 16-stamp sheet
Also appears on heavy, ungummed paper, and
16-stamp heavy paper sheet

1973: History of Olympics
1 Riyals
Also appears on 16-stamp sheet
Also appears on heavy, ungummed paper, and
16-stamp heavy paper sheet

1 Riyals – larger stamp
Also appears on three 1-stamp souvenir sheets:
rose, blue, and white borders
Also appears on 16-stamp sheet
Also appears on heavy, ungummed paper, and
16-stamp heavy paper sheet

United Arab Emirates

1988 Olympics
2.50 Dirhams

1992 Olympics
250 Fils

**1994: Centenary International
Olympic Committee**
1 Dirham
Bicycle symbol only

United Nations – Geneva

**1996: Sports and the Environment –
with Olympic Rings**
70 Centimes
Also appears on 2-stamp souvenir sheet

United States

1972 Olympics
6 Cents

1983: 1984 Olympics
35 Cents

1996 Olympics
32 Cents

Also appears on 20-stamp souvenir sheet

Upper Volta

1973: 1972 Olympics
1-stamp souvenir sheet – 500 Francs

1976 Olympics
1-stamp souvenir sheet – 500 Francs
Bicycle symbol only

1980 Olympics
65 Francs
Also appears on 1-stamp souvenir sheet
Also issued with "Soukhorouchenkov (URSS)"
overprint

150 Francs
Also appears on 1-stamp souvenir sheet
Also issued with "Hesslich (RDA)" overprint

250 Francs
Also appears on 1-stamp souvenir sheet
Also issued with "Lang (POL)" overprint

350 Francs
Also appears on 1-stamp souvenir sheet
Also issued with "Dill-Bundi (SUISSE)" overprint

1-stamp souvenir sheet – 500 Francs
Also issued with "Bondue (FRANCE)" overprint

Uruguay

1965: 1964 Olympics
80 Centesimos

Uzbekistan

1996 Olympics
20 Som

Vanuatu

1988 Olympics
2-stamp souvenir sheet – 150 Vatu
Bicycle in selvedge

Vietnam

1991: 1992 Olympics
400 Dong

1992 Olympics
1-stamp souvenir sheet – 10,000 Dong
Bicycle symbol only

1995: 1996 Olympics
3000 Dong

Wallis and Futuna Islands

1976 Olympics
31 Francs
Velodrome

Yemen (Kingdom)

1968: Commemorating 10 Olympic Games
4 Bogaches
Also appears on 1-stamp souvenir sheet

Yemen Arab Republic

1968 Olympics
50 Bogaches
No bicycle on stamp, "Gold Medals Daniel
Rebillard France" overprinted on chariot stamp
Also issued with "Gold Medals Pier Franco
Vianelli Italy" overprint

1971: Olympics Winners
⅓ Bogaches – Italy
2 Bogaches – France

1972: Olympic Winners
10 Bogaches – France
22 Bogaches – Italy

Yugoslavia

1960 Olympics
40 Dinar

1980 Olympics
3.40 Dinar

Zaire

1985: OLYMPHILEX '85
30 Zaire

Zambia

1992 Olympics
100 Kwacha

Zimbabwe

1984 Olympics
11 Cents

4

Bicycle Racing Stamps

It seems that as soon as two bicycles had been produced, people started racing them. The first recorded bicycle race, a 1,200 meter track competition, took place at Saint-Cloud, outside Paris, on 31 May 1868. The first official road race came 17 months later, a contest from Paris to Rouen, over 123 kilometers, with a field of 100 riders, including four women.

First Bicycle Racing Stamp

The first stamp to commemorate bicycle racing came from Bulgaria in 1931 for the Balkan Games, an event commemorated again by Bulgarian bicycle stamps in 1933 and 1947. The Balkan Games, an annual event held in the late summer or early winter, attracted competitors from Albania, Bulgaria, Greece, Romania, Turkey, and Yugoslavia. While a handful of women raced with the men in the world's first road race, a female didn't show up on a bicycle stamp until 90 years later — on a racing issue from China in 1959 celebrating the First National Games in Peking.

Popular Races

Some of the more popular bicycle racing events honored with postage stamps include the Tour de France, the Giro d'Italia, the World Championships (track, road, and cyclocross), and the International Bicycle Peace Race.

The Peace Race was first organized to help placate the somewhat strained relations between the peoples of Czechoslovakia and Poland after World War II. Co-sponsored by the leading newspapers in the two countries, Czechoslovakia's *Rude Pravo* and Poland's *Glos Ludu*, the riders in the multi-day stage race set out in 1948 on a course from Warsaw to Prague and back to Warsaw. In 1952 the race expanded to Berlin with East Germany's foremost newspaper *Neues Deutschland* becoming a co-sponsor.

The event's five-decade history saw over two dozen stamps issued by five Eastern Block countries. Russia produced the event's final postage stamp celebrating the Peace Race's 40th anniversary, in 1987.

The world's most famous bicycle race, the Tour de France, first appeared on a stamp in 1953 when the host country celebrated the Tour's 50th anniversary. However, France has yet to repeat a postal commemoration of its national cycling treasure.

Other nations have not been so shy. In 1972, Manama and Ajman, two of six Persian Gulf sheikdoms that have since formed the United Arab Emirates, both issued 20-stamp sets showing many of the top racers in that year's Tour de France, including the winner, Eddie Merckx. Also in 1972, Africa's Equatorial Guinea produced a set of seven stamps and two souvenir sheets commemorating the Tour. In addition, Tour de France commemorative stamp issuing countries include Monaco, the Netherlands, Tanzania, Luxembourg, and the tiny co-principality (France and Spain) of Andorra.

The Giro d'Italia, arguably the world's most grueling bike race, has been commemorated in postage stamps by four countries: the host nation, Italy, in 1967 for the

event's 50th anniversary, and then 25 years later for the 75th birthday; Ajman and Manama, each in 1972 with 20-stamp sets picturing some of the era's most famous cyclists; and by San Marino, in 1965, with a 3-stamp set — one stamp illustrates a stage start in front of the Government Palace, while the other two stamps show a field of cyclists racing down the road, Mt. Titano and the city of San Marino in the background.

The annual World Championships have been commemorated with bicycle stamps numerous times: the cyclo-cross championships by Italy and Luxembourg; and the road and track championships by a plethora of countries, including Canada, Venezuela, and Spain. The first one was Italy who hosted the 1951 races were held in Milan (track) and Varese (road). The Italy stamp shows a bicycle racer on a globe with the Milan Cathedral on his left and the bell tower of Varese on his right. No stamps have yet been issued commemorating the mountain bike World Championships, a newcomer to the World's scene, first officially contested in Crested Butte, Colorado in 1990.

In addition to the well-known cycling events, stamps have also honored bicycle racing as a part of China's National Farmers Games, the Southern Cross Games, the Southeast Asia Peninsular Games, Africa's Abidjan Games, and one competition that never took place.

In 1928, a "World Spartakiade" athletic event was discussed in the inner circles of the Soviet Union, "as a first step on the path to a world competition." The event, planned for 6–18 August 1933, in Moscow, hoped to draw 45,000 Soviet athletes, and 5,000 competitors from 37 foreign countries. The event's date kept getting pushed back, eventually into 1935. Ten commemorative stamps were issued that year, including Russia's first bicycle stamp. However, due to numerous difficulties, some having to do with stadium construction, the grandiose idea of a world competition in the capital of the "first workers' and peasants' state of the world" never materialized.

Track Racing

While road racing is the theme of the majority of the bicycle racing stamps issued, track racing and numerous velodromes have also been honored with stamps.

Venezuela issued a 4-stamp velodrome set in 1951 for the third Bolivian Games, while Cuba produced a 4-stamp set for the 1991 Pan American Games. The set showed various athletic venues, including the velodrome used during the competition. A 1970 Thailand stamp shows a velodrome that actually did double duty: after its first use for the 1964 Olympics in Tokyo, it was disassembled and moved to Bangkok for the 1966 Asian Games.

Velodromes have also been shown on stamps issued by Russia, Greece, the Wallis and Futuna Island, and a host of other countries.

Track racers have been shown on numerous stamps, as well. Some of the more attractive track racing stamps were issued by Canada (for the 1988 Commonwealth Games), East Germany (showing a team pursuit squad), Japan (for the 32nd National Athletic Meet — with Mt. Iwaki in the background), and North Korea (1980 Moscow Olympics).

Arguably the most striking track racing philatelic item was a souvenir sheet produced by the African nation of Guinea-Bissau. The lone stamp on the sheet illustrates a speeding track cyclist, while the souvenir sheet selvedge shows the outside of the 1976 Montreal Olympic velodrome.

Eddie Merckx

While most bicycle racing stamps show a "generic" racer, some actually picture an actual rider. Belgium's Eddie Merckx — winner of the Tour de France and the Giro d'Italia five times each, 3-time World Champion, former 1-hour record holder, winner of over 500 bicycle races, and arguably the world's best bicycle racer ever — has appeared on at least five stamps and two souvenir sheets.

Triathlon

Probably the most bizarre bicycle racing stamp story has to do with the sport of triathlon and one of its most eccentric participants: John E. duPont. DuPont, one of the heirs to the DuPont chemical company fortune, and accused murderer of Dave Schultz (1984 Olympic Gold Medalist in wrestling), started collecting stamps in the 1960s. In 1980, he purchased a rare British Guiana stamp for $935,000 at auction. DuPont reportedly was so excited about the acquisition that he flew the stamp in a helicopter around the Statue of Liberty and slept with it under his pillow.

After becoming involved in the sport of triathlon (sponsoring a plethora of events and teams to the tune of over $500,000) in the 1980s, duPont decided to finance the production of a souvenir sheet showing him swimming, bicycling and running. The sheet boldly proclaimed duPont as the "Father of Triathlon in the Americas" with the uninhabited island of Redonda, a dependency of Antigua in the West Indies, chosen as the issuing entity. DuPont spent $10,000 on the project. The postally valid $5 sheet, released in 1987 at CAPEX, an international stamp exhibition in Toronto, can still be used today as postage in Antigua and Barbuda.

Other stamps commemorating triathlon that carry the image of a cyclist were issued in 1995 by two French Territories: New Caledonia, in the South Pacific, celebrating the 10th Sunshine Triathlon, and St. Pierre & Miquelon, a group of islands off the southern coast of Newfoundland.

Listing of Stamps

Ajman

1969: Giro d'Italia
1 Dirhams – Eddy Merckx
2 Dirhams – Rudi Altig
5 Dirhams – Julio Jimenez
10 Dirhams – Felice Gimondi
15 Dirhams – Jan Jansen
20 Dirhams – Jaques Anquetil
12 Riyals – Tommy Simpson

All stamps in above set each appear on 1-stamp souvenir sheets

1-stamp souvenir sheet - 12 Riyals

1972: Tour de France
5 Dirhams – Baldini
10 Dirhams – Baldini
15 Dirhams – Riviere
20 Dirhams – Riviere
25 Dirhams – Wolfshohl
30 Dirhams – Wolfshohl
35 Dirhams – Bahamontes
40 Dirhams – Bahamontes
45 Dirhams – Altig
50 Dirhams – Motta
55 Dirhams – Poulidor
60 Dirhams – Aimar
65 Dirhams – Pingeon
70 Dirhams – Pingeon
75 Dirhams – Gimenez
80 Dirhams – Gimenez
85 Dirhams – Van Springel
90 Dirhams – Ocana
95 Dirhams – Merckx
1 Riyal – Merckx
All stamps in above set issued in both gold and silver borders
All stamps in above set also appear on 20-stamp sheet (both gold and silver)

Albania

1969: Spartakiad Games
80 Quintar

1989: Spartakiad Games
1 Lek

1993: Mediterranean Sea Games
21 Lek

Algeria

1978: 3rd African Games
40 Centimes
Bicycle symbol only

Andorra, French

1980 World Cycling Championships
1.20 Franc

1993 Tour de France
2.50 Franc

Angola

1981: 2nd Central African Games
50 Lweys

Argentina

1995 Pan American Games
75 Centavos

Austria

1987 World Championships
5 Schillings

Belgium

1969 World Road Championships
6 Francs

Benin

1978: 3rd African Games
60 Francs
80 Francs
Both stamps also appear on 3-stamp souvenir
sheet

Bolivia

1951: 5th Athletic Championship Matches
4 Boliviano
Also appears on 3-stamp souvenir sheet

1980: 1979 Southern Cross Games
2-stamp souvenir sheet
Bicycle symbol in selvedge

1993: 12th Bolivian Games
2.30 Boliviano
Bicycle symbol on flag

Bulgaria

1931: Balkan Games
10 Lek

1933: Balkan Games
10 Lek

1947: Balkan Games
2 Lek

1957: 4th Egyptian bicycle race
80 Stotinki – Brown stamp
80 Stotinki – Green stamp

1960: 10th Tour of Bulgaria Bicycle Race
1 Lek

1970: 20th Tour of Bulgaria Bicycle Race
20 Stotinki

1993 World Summer Games for Deaf
3 Lek

Burma

1961: 2nd Southeast Asia Peninsular Games
1 Kyat

Cameroun

1964: Tropics Cup Games
18 Francs

Canada

1974 World Cycling Championships
8 Cents

1994 British Commonwealth Games
88 Cents

Central Africa

1962: Abidjan Games
50 Francs

Chile

1991 Pan American Games
100 Peso

China, Peoples Republic

1957: 1st National Workers' Sports Meeting
8 Fen

1959: 1st National Sports Meeting
8 Fen

1965: 2nd National Games
10 Fen

1985: 2nd National Worker's Games
8 Fen

1988: 1st National Farmers' Games
8 Fen

Colombia

1957: 7th Tour of Colombia
2 Centavo
5 Centavo

1971 Pan American Games
1.30 Peso – Cyclist
1.30 Peso – Velodrome, yellow logo
1.30 Peso – Velodrome, red logo
1.30 Peso – Velodrome, green logo
1.30 Peso – Velodrome, blue logo
Above stamps also appear on 25-stamp sheet

1977: 13th Central American & Caribbean Games
6 Peso
Bicycle symbol on tab

1978: 13th Central American and Caribbean Games
10 Peso
Also appears on 16-stamp sheet

1992: 14th National Games
Sheet – Alligator on bicycle in sheet margin

1995: World BMX Championships
400 Peso

1995 World Cycling Championships
400 Peso

Congo, Peoples Republic

1965: 1st African Games
100 Francs
Also appears on 5-stamp souvenir sheet

1975: 10th Anniversary of 1st African Games
30 Francs

1976: 1st Central African Games
35 Francs

Cook Islands

1974: 10th British Commonwealth Games
30 Cents

Costa Rica

1984: 20th International Bicycle Race
6 Colon

Cuba

1969: 6th Socialist Bicycle Race
13 Centavos

1989: 1991 Pan American Games
5 Peso

1991: PANAMFILIX '91, 11th Pan American Games
50 Centavos
Velodrome

Czechoslovakia

1953: 6th International Peace Race
3 Koruna

1956: 9th International Peace Race
30 Haleru

1957: 10th International Peace Race
2-stamp set

1962: 15th International Peace Race
30 Haleru

1965 World Track Championships
60 Haleru

1967: 20th International Peace Race
60 Haleru

1977: 30th International Peace Race
4-stamp bicycle set

1987 World Cyclo-Cross Championships
6 Koruna

Dominican Republic

1973: 12th Central American & Caribbean Games
2 Centavos
8 Centavos
10 Centavos
25 Centavos

1974: 12th Central American and Caribbean Games
6 Centavos
Velodrome and bicycle symbol

1979: 8th Pan American Games
3 Centavos

1981: 5th National Games
50 Centavos

1983: 9th Pan American Games
15 Centavos

1983: 6th National Games
6 Centavos

1990: 9th National Games
10 Centavos

1991: 11th Pan American Games
50 Centavos

Ecuador

1965: 5th Bolivarian Games
2.50 Sucre
Also re-valued at 80 Centavos with
"$0,80" overprint

4 Sucre
Both stamps also appear on 12-stamp
souvenir sheet

1975: 3rd Ecuadorian Games
40 Centavos

1994 Junior Cycling Championships
300 Sucre
400 Sucre

Egypt

1958: 5th International Cycle Race
10 Milliemes

1991: 5th Africa Games
10 Piasters

Equatorial Guinea

1973: Tour de France
1 Peseta – Duyndam, Holland
2 Peseta – Teirlinck, Belgium
3 Peseta – Huysmans, Belgium
5 Peseta – Hezard, France
8 Peseta – Van Linden, Belgium
15 Peseta – Thevenet, France
50 Peseta – Merckx, Belgium

Two souvenir sheets listed with Semi-Postals
(see Chapter 5)

Estonia

1993 Baltic Sea Games
2 Kroon

France

1953: 50th Anniversary Tour de France
12 Francs

1972 World Cycling Championships
1 Franc

1989 World Cycling Championships
2.20 Francs

German Democratic Republic

1952: 5th International Peace Race
12 Pfennig

1953: 6th International Peace Race
3-stamp bicycle set

1954: 7th International Peace Race
2-stamp bicycle set

1955: 8th International Peace Race
2-stamp bicycle set

1956: 9th International Peace Race
2-stamp bicycle set

1957: 10th International Peace Race
5 Pfennig
No bicycle on stamp, map of race course

1962: 15th International Peace Race
2-stamp bicycle set

1967: 20th International Peace Race
2-stamp bicycle set

1969 World Cycling Championships
20 Pfennig

1977: 30th International Peace Race
3-stamp bicycle set

1979: 7th Children & Youth Spartakiad
10 Pfennig

Great Britain

1970: 9th British Commonwealth Games
1 Shilling 9 Pence

Greece

1986: 6th International Round-Europe Cycling Meet
50 Drachma

Grenada

1975 Pan American Games
2 Dollars

Guatemala

1964: 8th Bicycle Race
1 Centavo
2 Centavos
3 Centavos
4 Centavos
Above 4 stamps show no bicycle, overprinted with "VIII Vuelta Ciclistica"

1968: 11th Bicycle Race
4 Centavos
5 Centavos
6 Centavos
Above 3 stamps show no bicycle, Overprinted with "Aereo XI Vuelta Ciclistica 1967"

India

1982: 9th Asian Games
50 Paise

1991: 11th Asian Games
4 Rupees

Indonesia

1958: Bicycle Tour of Java
3-stamp bicycle set

1962: 4th Asian Games
15 Rupiah

1993: National Sport Week in Jakarta
300 Rupiah

Iran

1974: 7th Asian Games
1-stamp souvenir sheet – 10 Rials
Bicycle symbol only

1974: 7th Asian Games
2 Rials

Isle of Man

1978: 11th British Commonwealth Games
7 Pence

1986: 13th British Commonwealth Games
34 Pence

Israel

1975: 10th Hapoel Games – 50th Anniv.
1.70 Shekel

Italy

1951 World Cycling Championships
25 Lira

1962 World Cycling Championships
3-stamp bicycle set

1967: 50th Anniversary of the Giro d'Italia
3-stamp bicycle set

1968 World Cycling Championships
2-stamp bicycle set

1971 Youth Games
50 Lira

1979 World Cyclo-Cross Championships
2-stamp bicycle set

1985 World Cycling Championships
400 Lira

1992 Giro d'Italia
750 Lira (left half); 750 Lira (right half)

Jamaica

1962: 9th Central American and Caribbean Games
1 Pound
Also appears on 4-stamp souvenir sheet

1966: 8th British Empire and Commonwealth Games
6 Pounds
Also appears on 4-stamp souvenir sheet

Japan

1948: 3rd National Athletic Meet
5 Yen

1967 World University Games
50 Yen

1977: 32nd National Athletic Meeting
20 Yen

1990 World Cycling Championships
62 Yen

Kenya

1987: 4th All Africa Games
3 Cents

Khor Fakkan

1965 Pan-Arab Games
50 Naye Paise
Also issued revalued with "20Dh" overprint

Korea, North

1960: Liberation Day Sport Meet
5 Chun

Korea, South

1981: 62nd National Sports Festival
40 Won

1986 Asian Games
1-stamp souvenir sheet – 550 Won
Bicycle symbol only

Lebanon

1964: 4th Mediterranean Games
2.50 Pound

Libya

1967: 5th Mediterranean Games
15 Milliemes

1976 Arab Games
15 Dirham
30 Dirhams
100 Dirhams
Small bicycle on each stamp

1979 Junior World Cycling Championships
2-stamp bicycle set
The above stamps also appear on 1-stamp and
4-stamp souvenir sheets

1979 Mediterranean Games
15 Dirhams
Bicycle symbol only

30 Dirhams
Bicycle symbol only

70 Dirhams
Bicycle symbol only

Luxembourg

1952 World Cycling Championships
4 Francs

1962 World Cyclo-Cross Championships
2-stamp bicycle set

1989 Tour de France
9 Francs

Macao

1990 Asian Games
80 Avos
Also appears on 5-stamp souvenir sheet

Malaysia

1986: Malaysian Games
40 Cents
Bicycle symbol only

1989: 15th Southeast Asia Games
10 Cents

1995: 1996 British Commonwealth Games
1 Dollar

Malta

1993: 5th Games of Small States
4 Cents
Also appears on 4-stamp souvenir sheet

Manama

1969: Giro d'Italia
1 Dirhams – Eddy Merckx
2 Dirhams – Rudi Altig
5 Dirhams – Julio Jimenez
10 Dirhams – Felice Gimondi
15 Dirhams – Jan Jansen
20 Dirhams – Jaques Anquetil
12 Riyals – Tommy Simpson
All stamps in above set each appear on 1-stamp
souvenir sheets

1-stamp souvenir sheet – 12 Riyals

1972: Tour de France
5   Dirhams – Bartali
10 Dirhams – Coppi
15 Dirhams – Coppi
20 Dirhams – Bobet
25 Dirhams – Bobet
30 Dirhams – Koblet
35 Dirhams – Koblet
40 Dirhams – Kuebler
45 Dirhams – Kuebler
50 Dirhams – Darrigade
55 Dirhams – Darrigade
60 Dirhams – Anglade
65 Dirhams – Anglade
70 Dirhams – Ch. Gaul
75 Dirhams – Gemiani

80 Dirhams – Gemiani
85 Dirhams – Van Looy
90 Dirhams – Van Looy
95 Dirhams – Anquetil
1   Riyal – Anquetil
All stamps in above set issued in both gold and silver borders
All stamps in above set also appear on 20-stamp sheet (both gold and silver)

Mauritius

1985: 2nd Annual Indian Ocean Islands Games
1.25 Rupee

Monaco

1963: 50th Anniversary of Tour de France
2-stamp bicycle set

Morocco

1983 Mediterranean Games
80 Centimes
Bicycle symbol only
Also appears on 3-stamp souvenir sheet

Netherlands

1996: Tour de France
80 Cents

New Caledonia

1970: 4th Bicycle Race of New Caledonia
40 Francs

1995: 10th Sunshine Triathlon
60 Francs

New Zealand

1974: 10th British Commonwealth Games
10 Cents

1989: 14th British Commonwealth Games
80 Cents

Nicaragua

1982: 14th Central American and Caribbean Games
10 Centavos

Niger

1962: 10th Abidjan Games
15 Francs

Norway

1993 World Cycling Championships
5.50 Krone

Panama

1986: 15th Central American and Caribbean Games
23 Centavos

1987 Pan American Games
60 Centavos

Philippines

1965: 2nd Asian Cycling Championships
3-stamp bicycle set

1981: 11th Southeast Asian Games
1 Peso

1988: Tour of Mindanao
11 Peso

1993: 17th Southeast Asian Games
2 Peso

Poland

1948: 1st International Peace Race
15 Zloty

1948: 7th Poland Bicycle Race
3-stamp set

1952: 5th International Peace Race
40 Zloty

1953: 6th International Peace Race
3-stamp bicycle set

1954: 7th International Peace Race
2-stamp bicycle set

1955: 8th International Peace Race
2-stamp bicycle set

1956: 9th International Peace Race
2-stamp bicycle set

1957: 10th International Peace Race
2-stamp bicycle set

1962: 15th International Peace Race
3-stamp bicycle set

1967: 20th International Peace Race
60 Groszy

1972: 25th International Peace Race
60 Groszy

1977: 30th International Peace Race
1.50 Zloty

1986 World Cycling Championships
20 Zloty

Redonda

1987: CAPEX' '87
1-stamp souvenir sheet – 5 Dollars
Triathlete John E. duPont

Romania

1951 Bicycle Tour of Romania
11 Lei

1957: 10th International Peace Race
2-stamp set

1986: National Cycling Championships
4-stamp set

1-stamp souvenir sheet – 10 Lei

Russia

1935: International Spartacist Games
10 Kopecks

1956: All Union Spartacist Games
40 Kopecks

1957: 10th International Peace Race
40 Kopecks

1962: International Summer Sports Championships
2 Kopecks

1963: 3rd Spartacist Games
3 Kopecks
Also appears on 4-stamp souvenir sheet

1965: 8th Trade Union Spartacist Games
4 Kopecks

1965: 9th Spartacist Games for Children
6 Kopecks

1967: 4th Spartacist Games Commemorating 50th Anniversary of USSR
4 Kopecks

1986: 39th International Peace Race
10 Kopecks

1987: 40th International Peace Race
10 Kopecks

1990 Goodwill Games
10 Kopecks

Saar

1955 World Cyclo-Cross Championships
15 Francs

Salvador, El

1977: 2nd Central American Games
40 Centavos
1-stamp poster with bicycle in selvedge

1994: 22nd Tour of El Salvador
80 Centavos

Saint Pierre & Miquelon

1995: Triathlon
5.10 Francs

San Marino

1953: Turin University Sports Meet
4 Lira

1965: 48th Tour of Italy
3-stamp bicycle set

1985 Olympiad of Small States
450 Lira

1987: Mediterranean Games
700 Lira
Bicycle symbol only

1995 Junior World Cycling Championships
100 Lira

Seychelles

1993: 4th Indian Ocean Island Games
3.50 Rupee

Singapore

1973: 7th South East Asia Games
10 Cents
15 Cents
25 Cents
35 Cents
50 Cents
1 Dollar
No bicycle on stamps, "Cycling" listed as sport
Above stamp set also appear on 6-stamp
souvenir sheet

Slovakia

1996: Round Slovakia Cycle Race
3 Koruna

Slovenia

1996 World Junior Cycling Championships
55 Paras

Spain

1984 World Cycling Championships
17 Peseta

1990 World Cyclo-Cross Championships
20 Peseta

Tanzania

1990 Tour de France
30 Shillings

Thailand

1966: 5th Asian Games
20 Satangs

1970: 6th Asian Games
1.50 Baht
Velodrome

1975: 8th Southeast Asian Pacific Games
3 Baht
Also appears on 4-stamp souvenir sheet

1985: 13th Southeast Asian Pacific Games
5-stamp souvenir sheet
Siamese cat on bicycle in selvedge

Togo

1969: Inauguration of Omnisport Stadium
90 Francs
Also appears on 2-stamp souvenir sheet

Tunisia

1967 Mediterranean Games
10 Millimes
Bicycle symbol only

Turkey

1971 Mediterranean Games
250 Kurush

Turks & Caicos Islands

1978: 11th British Commonwealth Games
2 Dollars

Uganda

1978 British Commonwealth Games
4-stamp souvenir sheet
Bicycle symbol in selvedge

United States

1996: Bicycle Racing
2-stamp souvenir sheet
Also issued with "Tour of China '96" overprint

Upper Volta

1962: Abidjan Games
25 Franc

Uruguay

1969: 1968 World Cycling Championships
2-stamp bicycle set

Venezuela

1951: 3rd Bolivarian Games
4-stamp set – velodrome
All 4 stamps also appear on 4-stamp
souvenir sheet

1962: 1st National Games
40 Centimos
Also appears on 3-stamp sheet

1978: 1977 World Cycling Championships
2-stamp bicycle set

1983 Pan American Games
1 Bolivar
2.70 Bolivar
Both stamps also appear on 5-stamp
souvenir sheet

Wallis and Futuna Islands

1989 World Cycling Championships
10 Francs

5

Semi-Postals

In addition to the price of postage, stamps have at times carried surcharges to raise money for various organizations and causes within the issuing country. These stamps are called semi-postals.

The idea for semi-postals or "charity stamps," as they were first called, began in 1897 when New South Wales issued two stamps that bore a surcharge to raise money for consumptives' homes (people afflicted with pulmonary tuberculosis). Since then, semi-postals have become popular amongst numerous stamp issuing countries including over two dozen nations that have issued the surcharged-stamps featuring a bicycle.

European Semi-Postals

Germany has had a long history of semi-postal stamps showing a bike. Between West Germany (German Federal Republic), East Germany (German Democratic Republic), Germany–West Berlin, and united Germany, 25 semi-postal bicycle stamps have been issued.

The first German semi-postal bike stamp, issued in a 2-stamp set in 1949, commemorates the Tour of Germany bicycle race. The two stamps are identical except for different colors (one is brown, the other green), and two different values: 10 + 5

pfennig and 20 + 10 pfennig. The stamps helped raise money for the race.

Another German semi-postal set, issued by East Germany in 1964, commemorates six famous Germans killed by the Nazis. The three cycling stamps in the 6-stamp set show a group of Nazi resisters posting and painting anti-Hitler and anti-pacifist slogans on the side of a building. Each stamp contains a portrait of a victim. The three men shown on the cycling issues are Anton Saefkow, Franz Jacob, and Bernhard Bastleim, all members of the so-called Red Orchestra, an underground resistance group that operated during Hitler's reign.

A year earlier, East Germany commemorated another Nazi victim, Albert Richter, a famous German cyclist. Richter, 1932 World Amateur Sprint Champion, tried to escape from Germany with money hidden in his sew-up tires. On a tip, the Nazis caught Richter and discovered his money. He died shortly after being interrogated. The 15 + 5 pfennig stamp's surcharge went to the maintenance of East German memorials. A velodrome in Cologne was dedicated to Richter's memory in 1996. Germany's latest bicycle semi-postal commemorates 1995 Stamp Day.

Belgium produced a 4-stamp semi-postal set in 1963 featuring track and road racing. The stamps, issued to commemorate the 80th anniversary of the Belgian Bicycle League, carried a surcharge from 50 centimes to 1 franc. The monies collected from the stamp sales helped support the 1964 Belgium Olympic team. A special postal card commemorating the 1964 Tokyo Olympics and carrying the five-color Olympic rings was produced, as well, showing the stamps as imperfs. Belgium also issued bicycle semi-postals in 1968, 1980, and 1988.

The Netherlands and the Netherlands Antilles together have issued over a dozen bicycle semi-postal stamps. Dutch surcharges usually support the country's child welfare programs or various social and cultural institutions. In addition to the semi-postals, sometimes special "Thank You" cards bearing likenesses of the stamps are produced and distributed to schools, places

of business, and local committees who
helped promote charity stamp sales.

Asian Semi-Postals

Semi-postal issues are not just concentrated
in Europe. In Asia, a number of countries
have produced semi-postals, several of
them showing a bicycle. Laos issued a 3-
stamp set in 1967 with the additional monies collected helping the victims of the
devastating Mekong Delta flood of 1966.
The stamps also came out on a souvenir
sheet. One of the stamps shows someone
pushing a bicycle through a flooded village,
the water practically covering the bike's bottom bracket.

South Korea produced a series of Olympic semi-postal stamps and souvenir sheets
to help finance the country's hosting of the
1988 Seoul Olympics. Twelve Maximum
Cards were also issued. Each colorful card
carries the 1988 Seoul Olympic logo, an illustration of the stamp, the semi-postal
stamp, and a fancy cancel of Hodori the Tiger Cub participating in a particular sport.
The bicycle card pictures the mascot racing
a bike.

Thailand issued a semi-postal stamp in
1989 illustrating the downside of bicycle
racing — crashing. On the 2+1 baht denomination stamp a cyclist is shown after a
wreck: down on the track, shoes off, bike
behind him, and a nurse administering to
his wrist some kind of salve from a bottle.
The surcharge was slated for "sports welfare." Another Thailand "sports welfare"
semi-postal stamp, issued in 1991, shows a
family of four cycling in a park on three
bikes (one of the participant is riding atop
the rear rack of one of the bicycles).

Semi-Postal Overprints

Sometimes a normal stamp becomes a semi-
postal when it is re-issued with an overprinted surcharge.

On 12 September 1988, Hurricane Gilbert struck Jamaica, causing an estimated
$1.3 billion in damage (including practi-

cally all of the country's banana plantations), killing 30 people, and displacing 20 percent of the population. Jamaica's Prime Minister called it the worst disaster in Jamaica's modern history. The postal service reissued a set of 1988 Olympic stamps, including the bicycle design, with a 45-cent surcharge, and earmarked the monies for hurricane relief.

Eight years earlier, St. Vincent overprinted an Olympic set, including a bicycle stamp, with a 50-cent surcharge to help the island rebuild after Hurricane Allen hit. And in 1958, the Dominican Republic overprinted a 5-stamp Olympic set, first issued after the Games in 1957, with a 2-cent surcharge to raise money for the United Nations Relief and Works Agency for Palestine Refugees.

Listing of Stamps

Algeria

1958: Motorized Mail Distribution
15 Francs + 5 Francs
"Algerie" overprint on 1958 France stamp

Argentina

1963: 4th Pan American Games
11 Peso + 5 Peso

Austria

1990: Stamp Day
7 Schilling + 3 Schilling
Scouting bicycle merit badge

Belgium

1963: 80th Anniversary of Belgium Bicycle League
1 Franc + 50 Centimes
2 Francs + 1 Franc
3 Francs + 1.50 Franc
6 Francs + 3 Francs
Surcharge for athletes at 1964 Olympics
All 4 stamps also appear on 4-stamp sheet printed on thick paper

1968: 1968 Olympics
6 Francs + 2 Francs

1982: Sports
9 Francs + 4 Francs
Also appears on 4-stamp souvenir sheet, however the stamp is printed in a different color, and revalued at 25 Francs

1988 Olympics
13 Francs + 3 Francs

Domincan Republic

1958
7 Centavos + 2 Centavos
7 Centavos + 5 Centavos
Overprint of 1956 Olympic stamp
Issued each with Star of David and crescent moon
+5 stamps each also appear on 5-stamp
souvenir sheets
Surcharge for U.N. Relief and Work Agency for
Palestine Refugees

Equatorial Guinea

1972 Olympics
1-stamp souvenir sheet – 250 + 50 Peseta
Bicycle symbol in selvedge

1972 Tour de France
1-stamp souvenir sheet – 250 + 50 Peseta
Merckx and Gimondi

France

1958: Motorized Mail Distribution
15 Francs + 15 Francs

1972: Stamp Day 1972
50 Centimes + 10 Centimes

1993: Stamp Day
2.50 Franc + 60 Centimes

France – Reunion

1972: Stamp Day
25 Francs + 5 Francs
"25+5 CFA" overprint of 1972 France stamp

German Democratic Republic

1960 World Championships
20 Pfennig + 10 Pfennig
25 Pfennig + 10 Pfennig

1962: 15th International Peace Race
20 Pfennig + 10 Pfennig

1963: Sportsmen Victims of the Nazis
15 Pfennig + 5 Pfennig
Surcharge for maintenance of national memorials

1964: Members of the Red Orchestra
5 Pfennig + 5 Pfennig
10 Pfennig + 5 Pfennig
15 Pfennig + 5 Pfennig
Surcharge for the support of memorials for
Nazi victims

1969: 6th Liepzig Sportsfest
20 Pfennig + 5 Pfennig
Surcharge for German Gymnastic and
Sports League

1988: 1988 Olympics
50 Pfennig + 20 Pfennig

Germany

1949: Bicycle Tour of Germany
10 Pfennig + 5 Pfennig
20 Pfennis + 10 Pfennig

1972 Olympics
25 Pfennig + 10 Pfennig
Velodrome
Also appears on 4-stamp souvenir sheet
Surcharge for Promotion of 1972 Olympics

1985: International Year of the Child
50 Pfennig + 20 Pfennig
60 Pfennig + 30 Pfennig
80 Pfennig + 40 Pfennig
120 Pfennig + 60 Pfennig
Surcharge to benefit young people

1991 World Cycling Championships
100 Pfennig + 50 Pfennig
Surcharge for Promotion of Sports

1991: Post Offices
30 Pfennig +15 Pfennig

1995: Stamp Day
200 Pfennig + 100 Pfennig

Germany W. Berlin

1978: Sport
50 Pfennig + 25 Pfennig
Surcharge for German Sports Foundation

1984 Olympics
80 Pfennig + 40 Pfennig
Surcharge for German Sports Foundation

1985: International Year of the Child
50 Pfennig + 20 Pfennig
60 Pfennig + 30 Pfennig
80 Pfennig + 40 Pfennig
120 Pfennig + 60 Pfennig
Surcharge for benefit of young people

Grenada Grenadines

1986: 1988 Olympics
10 Cents + 5 Cents

Hungary

1941: Military
40 Filler + 60 Filler
Surcharge for the benefit of the army

1953: Stamp Day
1 Forint + 1 Forint
2 Forint + 2 Forint

Ifni

1958: Sports
15 Centimos + 5 Centimos
Surcharge for child welfare

Indonesia

1995: 10th Asia & Pacific Regional Conference of Rehabilitation International
700 Rupiah + 100 Rupiah
"Mother's Love" painting by disabled
artist Patricia Saerang

Jamaica

1988 Olympics
45 Cents + 45 Cents
"Hurricane Gilbert Relief Fund" and 45 Cent
surcharge overprinted in both red and black on
1988 Olympics stamp

Japan

1963: 1964 Olympics
5 Yen + 5 Yen
Also appears on 4-stamp souvenir sheet

Korea, South

1985: 1988 Olympics
70 Won + 30 Won
Also appears on 2-stamp souvenir sheet
Surcharge for Olympic Games

Laos

1967: Mekong Delta Flood
40 Kip + 10 Kip
Also appears on 3-stamp sheet
Surcharge for victims of Mekong Delta flood

Lebanon

1960 Olympics
25 Pounds + 25 Pounds
Also appears on 3-stamp souvenir sheet
Also issued with "Chapionnat d'Europe..."
overprint for European Marksmanship
Championships

Netherlands

1958: Children's Games
4 Cents + 4 Cents
Tricycle
Surcharge for child welfare

1962: Children's Activities
6 Cents + 4 Cents
Surcharge for child welfare

1965: Children Artistic and Creative Activities
10 Cents + 6 Cents
Surcharge for child welfare

1974: Designs
30 Cents + 10 Cents
Surcharge for various social and
cultural institutions

1976: 75th Anniversary Social Insurance Bank
55 Cents + 20 Cents
Surcharge for various social and cultural institutions

1980: 75th Anniversary Promotion of Nature Preserves
80 Cents + 35 Cents
Surcharge for social and cultural purposes

1991: Dutch Farms
55 Cents + 30 Cents
Surcharge for social and cultural welfare organizations

1991: Children Playing
70 Cents + 30 Cents
6-stamp souvenir sheet
Bicycle in selvedge

Netherlands Antilles

1978: Children's Activities
40 Cents + 18 Cents
Surcharge for child welfare

1982: Sports
85 Cents + 40 Cents
Surcharge for sporting events

1990: Youth Care Campaign
65 Cents + 15 Cents
Surcharge for Antillean Youth Care Federation

New Zealand

1995: Children's Health
80 Cents + 5 Cents
Also appears on 4-stamp souvenir sheet
Souvenir sheet also issued with STAMPEX '95 logo

1996: Children's Health
4-stamp souvenir sheet
Bicycle in selvedge

Panama

1961: 1960 Olympics
10 Centavos + 1 Centavos
"Rehabilitacion de Menor" and 1 Centavos
Surcharge overprinted on 1960 Olympic stamp

Philippines

1959: World Scout Jamboree
30 Centavos + 10 Centavos
Also appears on 5-stamp souvenir sheet
Surcharge for 10th Boy Scout World Jamboree

Poland

1976 Olympics
1-stamp souvenir sheet
10 Zloty + 5 Zloty
bicycle in selvedge

Russia

1977: 1980 Olympics
4 Kopecks + 2 Kopecks

Saint Vincent

1980: Sports for All
60 Cents + 50 Cents
"Hurricane Relief 50C" overprint on 1980
Olympic stamp

Spain

1989: 1992 Olympics
20 Peseta + 5 Peseta

Spanish Guinea

1959: Stamp Day
10 Centimos + 5 Centimos
20 Centimos + 5 Centimos
50 Centimos + 20 Centimos

Thailand

1989: Sports Welfare
2 Baht + 1 Baht
Surcharge for sports welfare organizations

1991: Sports
2 Baht + 1 Baht
Surcharge for sports welfare organizations

6

Postal Carriers

"Neither snow, nor rain, nor heat, nor gloom of night stays these couriers from the swift completion of their appointed rounds." So goes the unofficial motto for the United States Postal Service. No mention is made of a dropped chain, or a flat bicycle tire.

Postal services around the world have used every means of transportation available to deliver the mail, from trains to schooners to bikes. In fact, the first bicycle stamps issued by a dozen countries including Cuba, Panama, Philippines, the United States, and Vietnam show a postal carrier.

Of the forty or so stamps issued with postal carriers on bicycles, most picture workers pedaling conventional two-wheelers. However, four of the stamps — issued by Dominica, Togo, Germany, and Equatorial Guinea — illustrate non-conventional bikes and trikes used in postal delivery.

Unusual Postal Bikes

In 1990, Dominica, in the West Indies, issued a 6-stamp set (including a cycling stamp) commemorating "Stamp World London '90," an international philatelic gathering. The cycling stamp shows a bearded gentleman riding an 1883 Centre Cycle, nicknamed a "Hen and Chickens." The contraption received its moniker due to the

arrangement of the four smaller wheels (the chickens) teemed around the large center wheel (the hen). Invented by Edward Burstow, an architect from Horsham, Sussex, just south of London, the 5-wheeled cycle proved popular to the area's postmen. One postal worker even wrote Mr. Burstow a letter stating the "Centre Cycle is vastly superior in every respect to any other wheel machine." However, the design never caught on with the general public, and manufacture was summarily discontinued.

Togo also released a stamp illustrating the "Hen and Chickens" bicycle in 1979, commemorating the 75th anniversary of the death of Rowland Hill (the inventor of the adhesive postage stamp).

In 1897, Germany produced a postal carrier stamp showing three utility tricycles picking up mail from a train. The stamp commemorates Germany's 1987 Stamp Day, an annual philatelic celebration begun in 1975 by the Association of German Philatelists. It's interesting to note that the original 1987 Stamp Day design included a person on a motor scooter (remember: that was supposed to be in 1897?) but the offending vehicle was removed before final art approval.

Another interesting design appears on a 1974 Equatorial Guinea stamp. As part of a 7-stamp set entitled "Transportation from Messenger to Rocket," the bike illustrated is equipped with an auxilliary motor mounted above the front wheel, and what looks like a gas tank attached to the handlebars. The stamp set commemorates the 100th anniversary of the Universal Postal Union, or UPU, an organization of worldwide postal authorities who set international postage rates, handling of international mail, and other matters.

Women Postal Carriers

Women atop bicycles appear on only four postal carrier stamps: a 1966 Chinese issue picturing a female rural mail carrier; a 2-stamp 1953 semi-postal set from Hungary; and a 1988 Danish release of a postwoman

pedaling a bike laden with rear panniers and a large case attached to a front rack.

Boy Scouts

In 1991, the Grenadines of St. Vincent produced an interesting (even though not factually correct) postal carrier stamp, commemorating mail delivery by Czech boy scouts in the newly-formed nation of Czechoslovakia. From 7 through 25 November 1918, and again on 21 December, when Czechoslovakia's first president arrived, the boy scouts delivered registered mail, as per their contract with the country's National Committee. But the stamp pictures a scout placing mail in a letter box. Since registered mail requires a signed receipt, one wonders what the boy scout is doing. The stamp may also be in error in showing a bicycle. While the Czechoslovakian boy scouts may have used bicycles to perform their delivery duties, no documentation has been found to confirm their use.

Other Interesting Postal Carrier Stamps

Pity the poor bicycle postal carrier on the 500-lira value San Marino stamp. Issued to commemorate World Communication Year in 1983, the stamp has the postman riding a bicycle obviously too small for him. His knees almost hit the handlebars, and the seat is so low, he can barely extend his legs.

Every January since 1985, An Post, Ireland's official postal administration, begins each philatelic year by issuing a set of "Love" stamps. A heart is always included in at least one of the designs. The inaugural 2-stamp set shows a bouquet of heart flowers on one of the stamps. A 1990 issue pictures a heart-shaped hot air balloon, and a 1987 design shows a postman on a bicycle with hearts floating out of the letter bag on his back.

A 1991 Bulgarian issue also shows a postal carrier riding a bike; however mail, not hearts, are escaping from his mail bag and into the air. He doesn't seem concerned: he's smiling.

In Zambia, postal carriers take their mail-carrying seriously: A 1979 stamp, issued to commemorate the 100th anniversary of Rowland Hill's death, shows a mailman shouldering a rifle.

In Sri Lanka, one wonders if the nation's postal administration would have issued the 1992 "Postal Excellence" set of stamps if they had known that four years later the carriers would be striking over, not money, but new bicycle tires. The postal carriers in the northern section of the country stated they couldn't perform their duties because of bad tires and tubes. The government, hesitant to meet their demands for newer equipment, feared the tires and tubes would fall into liberation rebel hands. The rebels even issued a press release on behalf of the postmen stating, among other things, that the Sri Lankan government was negligent in their postal services to the people of the country.

Listing of Stamps

Barbados

1976: 125th Anniversary of Post Office Act
8 Cents

1984: Centenary Universal Postal Union
1-stamp souvenir sheet – 2 Dollars
Bicycle in selvedge

Benin

1978: Mail Delivery
60 Francs

1979: 20th Anniversary of Posts and Telecommunications
60 Francs

Bhutan

1970: New headquarters of United Postal Union in Bern, Switzerland
3 Chetrum
10 Chetrum
20 Chetrum
2.50 Ngultrum
Also issued revalued at 90 Chetrum
with overprint

Botswana

1974: 100th Anniversary of the Universal Postal Union
2 Cents

Brazil

1994: UPAE America '94
110 Cruzado

Bulgaria

1939: Postman on Bicycle
5 Lek – Blue stamp
20 Lek – Red stamp

1991: Philatelic Review Centennial
30 Stotinki

Cape of Good Hope

1900
1 Penny

Cayman Islands

1980: London '80 International Stamp Exhibition
40 Cents

Central Africa

1978: Sir Roland Hill
50 Francs
Also appears on 1-stamp souvenir sheet

China, Peoples Republic

1950: 1st All-China Postal Conference
400 Yuan
800 Yuan
Small bicycle on each stamp

1966: Rural Mail Carrier
8 Fen

Colombia

1994: Postal Vehicles
270 Peso
300 Peso
Bicycle on tab

Comoro Islands

1978: Sir Rowland Hill
30 Francs
Also appears on 1-stamp souvenir sheet

Croatia

1993: 1st United Postal Union Anniversary
1800 Dinar

Cuba

1899: Special Delivery
10 Centavos
"Immediata" misspelled

1902: Special delivery stamp
10 Centavos
1899 stamp re-issued with "Inmediata" corrected

1910: Special delivery
10 Centavos
Also issued with an inverted center

Dahomey

1967: Stamp Tax
3 Francs

Denmark

1988: Transport and Communication
3 Krone

Dominica

1990: Postal History
3 Dollars

Equatorial Guinea

1974: 100th Anniversary Universal Postal Union
30 Ekuele

France

1993: Stamp Day
2.50 Franc

German Democratic Republic

1953: Stamp Day
24 Pfennig

Germany, Federal Republik

1987: Stamp Day
80 Pfennig

Greece

1979: Mail Delivery
4 Drachma

Guernsey

1988: Transport and Communication
22 Pence
Front half of bicycle

22 Pence
Back half of bicycle

Guyana

1974: Centenary of Universal Postal Union
25 Cents
50 Cents

Indonesia

1964: Transportation and Communications
4 Rupiah

1974: Centennial of United Postal Union
20 Rupiah

Ireland

1983: World Communications Year
22 Pence

1987: Love
28 Pence

Ivory Coast

1961: Stamp day
25 Francs

Jamaica

1983: World Communications Year
45 Cents

Japan

1973: 5th Anniversary Postal Code System
20 Yen

1995: 70th Anniversary First Air Mail Service
110 Yen
Stamp on stamp

Malaysia

1992: Postal Transport
30 Cents

Maldive Islands

1979: Postal Scenes
1.50 Rafiyaa
Donald Duck on unicycle

Mexico

1994: Postal Transport Vehicles
2 Peso

New Zealand

1987: Establishment New Zealand Post Ltd.
40 Cents

Nigeria

1983: World Communications Year
10 Kobo

Norway

1996: Postal carrier
3.50 Krone

Panama

1929: Special Delivery
10 Centavos
20 Centavos
Each of above 2 stamps also issued
with 5 different overprints

Philippines

1907: Special Delivery
10 Cents
"Philippines" overprinted on 1902 U.S.
Special Delivery stamp

1947: Special Delivery
20 Centavos

Poland

1950: 3rd Congress of PTT Trade Unions
15 Zloty

Rhodesia

1974: Universal Postal Union Centenary
7½ Cents

Romania

1982: Stamp Day
2 Lei

1983: Stamp Day
1 Leu

1987: Stamp Day
1 Leu

Saint Vincent Grenadines

1991: Czech Scout Mail
2 Dollars

San Marino

1983: World Communications Year
500 Lira

Sri Lanka

1992: Postal Excellence
1 Rupee
10 Rupee
Stamp on stamp, small bicycle

1993: Postal Excellence
1 Rupee

Togo

1979: 75th Anniversary Death of Rowland Hill
100 Francs
Also appears on 2-stamp souvenir sheet

United States

1902: Special Delivery
10 Cents
5 varieties exist

Upper Volta

1967: Stamp Day
30 Francs

Vietnam

1983: World Communication Year
50 Xu

1986: Postal Carrier with Bicycle
2 Dong

Vietnam, South

1971: Rural Mail
20 Dong

Yemen Arab Republic

1981: Rowland Hill Commemoration
1-stamp souvenir sheet – 200 Fils

Zambia

1979: Rowland Hill Commemoration
32 Ngwee
Also issued with "London 1980" overprint
Both stamp and overprint each appear on
4-stamp souvenir sheets

**1985: 10th Anniversary Postal and
Telecommunications Corporation**
20 Ngwee
Also issued revalued at 2 Kwacha

1990: Stamp World London '90
1.20 Kwacha

Zimbabwe

1983: World Communications Year
9 Cents

7

Special Subjects

While stamps issued to commemorate the Olympics and bicycle racing make up the bulk of worldwide cycling stamps, bicycles can also be found in issues celebrating such diverse topics as art, transportation, health and safety, Christmas, the military, scouting, space travel, animals, and children.

Art

Every postage stamp is basically a tiny piece of art; after all, most stamps originate from an artist's brush (or pencil, or other medium). So it comes as no surprise that famous paintings have been reproduced on stamps. And some of them depict bicycles.

Saint Lucia issued a souvenir sheet in 1981 to commemorate the 100th anniversary of the birth of Pablo Picasso. Pictured on the stamp is Picasso's "Night Fishing at Antibes," which includes a portion of a stylized bicycle.

In 1986, France produced a 2.20-franc value stamp from Fernand Leger's "Les Loisirs" to commemorate the 50th anniversary of the French Popular Front, the alliance between Socialists and Communists of 1935. The painting shows a bicycle.

Mexico honored artist Antonio Ruiz in 1988 with three stamps produced from his paintings. One of the paintings, "Parade," includes a bicyclist in the crowd.

The painting "Farmers' Holiday" by Russian artist Sergei Vasilievich of the then Soviet Union, appeared on a 1967 Russian stamp, and became part of a 9-stamp set commemorating the 50th anniversary of the October Revolution.

Transportation

Many present-day automobile clubs began as bicycle clubs. Italy, The Netherlands, and Monaco have issued stamps to commemorate the bicycle/auto club connection. And before the motor taxi, came the bicycle rickshaw, or trishaw.

Over half a dozen stamps carry the image of the trishaw, all from Asian nations, except for a 1992 issue from Tanzania. The African nation's stamp, which shows Pope John Paul II riding in a trishaw, celebrated the Pope's 1986 trip to Bangladesh.

Singapore has produced the most stamps of bicycle-powered rickshaws. A 1971 "Tourism" set contains two trishaw designs, while a 1990 Tourism stamp shows a trishaw in front of the Raffles Hotel. The hotel is famous for the Singapore sling cocktail, first concocted there in 1915 by a bartender named Ngiam Tong Boon. Singapore also issued machine-vended labels picturing three trishaws, in 1992. Postage, sold in 5-cent increments up to $2, was purchased and added to the labels.

Health and Safety

Numerous stamps have been issued to promote the importance of health and safety. The Netherlands, Tonga, Nigeria, and Hungary have each produced a number of bicycle safety stamps, and Australia, Sweden, and Canada, an assortment of health stamps each.

The most graphic public awareness bicycle stamp, issued in 1978 by Bophuthatswana (a "Homeland" enclave within the Republic of South Africa), promotes "Road Safety." The stamp illustrates in full color an unconscious child lying underneath a car with his damaged trike in the background.

Animated Characters

Some countries — including Antigua, Grenada, Uganda and Gambia — have discovered a gold mine in selling stamps picturing Disney characters. A few of the stamps show the world's most famous rodent and his pals pictured on or with bicycles. Other animated critters illustrated on bike stamps include Olympic mascots, a Russian hare from a 1969 children's cartoon, and Dino, Fred Flintstone's pet dinosaur. Real life animals have appeared on bicycle stamps, as well, mostly through circus issues from Mongolia, Hungary, and East Germany.

Other Subjects

Russia produced four stamps showing cosmonauts preparing for, or living in, space. In all four, a cosmonaut is working out on a stationary bike. The 50th anniversary of World War II commemorative stamps from numerous countries show bicycles being ridden into battle or transported from ships. Numerous train issues have included bicycles in the designs. Of coure, some of the bicycles shown are so small that you may need a magnifying glass to discern them.

Listing of Stamps

Aland

1991: Couple on tandem
2.90 Markka

Albania

1971: Painting
1.20 Lek

1972: Painting
2 Lek

1981: Unicyclists
15 Quintar

1983: Sports
25 Quintar

Andorra, French

1994: Tourism
2.80 Francs

Anguilla

1992: Christmas
2.40 Dollar
Also appears on a 4-stamp souvenir sheet

1992: Easter
80 Cents

Antigua

1980: London International Stamp Exhibition
4 Cents
Huey, Dewey & Louie on triple bicycle

Antigua and Barbuda

1990: Stamp World '90
1-stamp souvenir sheet
6 Dollars

1991: Trains
60 Cents

1993: Disney Posters
2 Dollars

Argentina

1975: Tourism
1.20 Peso
Hay wagon followed by bicyclists

1996: Centenary of Cinema
75 Centavos
"Bicicletas" printed on stamp
Also appears on 6-stamp sheet

Australia

1936: Centenary of South Australia
2 Pence – Small bicycle, blue stamp
3 Pence – Small bicycle, green stamp
1 Shilling – Small bicycle, red stamp

1975: Road Safety
10 Cents

1980: Community Welfare
22 Cents

1985: Centenary District Nursing Service
33 Cents

1988: Living Together Series
40 Cents

1989: Sports
41 Cents
Also issued as a self-adhesive

1992: Christmas
45 Cents
Tricycle

Austria

1985
4 Schilling
Carnival figures riding high-wheelers

Bangladesh

1987: Transportation
3 Taka
Trishaw

Barbados

1976: 10th Anniversary of Independence
15 Cents
Also appears on 4-stamp souvenir sheet

1985: 150th Anniversary of Royal Barbados Police
25 Cents

1987: 75th Anniversary of National Scouting Movement
65 Cents
Bicycle merit badge

Barbuda

1991
1-stamp souvenir sheet – 6 Dollars
Overprint "Barbuda Mail" on Antigua & Barbuda souvenir sheet

Belgium

1982: Sports
4-stamp souvenir sheet
Corresponding stamp appears with semi-postals (Chapter 5)

1988: Tourism
9 Francs
Small bicycle

Belize

1980 London Stamp Show
25 Cents
Small bicycle
Also appears on 1 stamp souvenir sheet with stamp revalued at 15 Dollars

Benin

1978: Kanna Bicycle Taxi
50 Francs

1986
15 Franc over 45 Franc
Overprint of Dahomey 1968 stamp

Bermuda

1971: Keep Bermuda Beautiful
24 Cents
Small bicycle

1989: Ferry Service
50 Cents
Bicycle on ferry

1993: Tourism
25 Cents

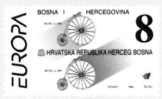

1994: Tourism
25 Cents
Small bicycle

Bhutan

1990: Stamp World London '90
1-stamp souvenir sheet – 30 Ngultrum
Fresno–San Francisco local post stamp in selvedge

Bosnia Herzegovina

1994: Europa
8 Dinar

Brazil

1983: Vaccination Campaign
30 Cruzado

British Virgin Islands

1979: International Year of the Child
1 Dollar
Also appears on 4-stamp souvenir sheet

Brunei

1971: 50th Anniversary of the Royal Brunei Police Force
15 Sen

Bulgaria

1946: 50th Anniversary of Bulgarian Postal Savings
4 Lek

1950: Sports
9 Lek

1969: Circus – bear on a bicycle
5 Stotinki

1978: Painting by Boris Ivanov
13 Stotinki
Also appears on 6-stamp sheet

Caicos Islands

1985: International Youth Year
1-stamp souvenir sheet – 2 Dollars
Bicycle in selvedge

Cameroun

1981: International Year of the Disabled
150 Franc
Hand-pedaled wheelchair

Canada

1989: Sesquicentennial of photography in Canada
38 Cents
High-wheelers in street

1994: World War II
43 Cents
Troops carrying bikes at D-Day

1994: World War II
43 Cents
Cyclist in crowd

Cayman Islands

1993: Tourism
30 Cents

Central Africa

1969: International Toy Fair
100 Francs
Small bicycle

1986: France–Central Africa Week
130 Francs

Chile

1996: Safety
10-stamp sheets

China

1947: Post office
1000 Yuan – Lilac stamp
1250 Yuan – Green stamp

China, Peoples Republic

1957: Peoples Liberation
8 Fen
Small bicycle

1974: Paintings by farmers of Huhsien County
8 Fen
Ssmall bicycle

1976: Fulfillment of 4th 5-Year Plan
8 Fen
Family with bicycle

8 Fen
Bicycle in store window

1976: Fulfillment of 4th 5-Year Plan
8 Fen
Small bicycle

1981: Quality Month
8 Fen – Silver medal, bicycle symbol
8 Fen – Gold medal, bicycle symbol

China, Republic of (Taiwan)

1985: 1st Anniversary Kaohsiung Cross-Harbor Tunnel
5 Yuan
Small bicycle

Christmas Island

1990: Transport through the Ages
10 Cents
Trishaw

1991: Island Police Force
43 Cents
Also appears on 4-stamp souvenir sheet

Colombia

1986: 25th Anniversary National Coffee Producers Assn. Sponsorship of National Cycling team
60 Peso

Congo, Peoples Republic

1961: Modern Transportation
5 Francs

1985: PHILEXAFRICA '85
10-stamp sheet
Cyclist on 5 tabs

Costa Rica

1984: Christmas
10 Centavos

Cuba

1962: National Sports Institute
2 Centavos
Also appears 5 times on 25-stamp sheet

1970: Road Safety Week
9 Centavos
Tricycle

Czech Republic

1993: Tourism
1 Koruna
Small bicycle

Czechoslovakia

1952: Unified Physical Education program
3 Koruna

1957: 700th Anniversary town of Moravska Trebova
1.25 Koruna
Small bicycle

1959: 50th Anniversary of Jan Kaspar's 1st flight in Czech plane
1.80 Koruna
Small bicycle

1963: 80th Anniversary Czechoslovakian Cycling
60 Haleru

Dahomey

1968: Postal Services
30 Francs
45 Francs

Denmark

1937: 25th Anniversary Accession to the Throne of King Christian X
10 Ore
Cyclists in background

30 Ore
Cyclists in background

1977: Road Safety Traffic Act
100 Ore

1985: Sports
6 Krone

1985: U.N. Decade for Women
3.80 Krone

1985: 300th Anniversary German and French Reform Church
2.80 Krone
Small bicycle

1987: HAFNIA '87 World Philatelic Exhibition
2-stamp souvenir sheet
Bicycle in selvedge

1990: Prevent Bicycle Theft
3.25 Krone

1996: Sports
9.60 Krone
Also appears on two 4-stamp souvenir sheets
contained in a mini-sheet booklet

Djibouti

1983: Manned Flight Bicentenary
1 stamp souvenir sheet
45 Francs
Bicycle in selvedge

Dominca

1992: Day of the Elderly
45 Cents

1993: Bangkok Expo
25 Cents

1996: Year of the Rat
1-stamp souvenir sheet – 3 Dollars

Ethiopia

1962: 3rd Africa Football Cup
20 Cents

Faroe Islands

1996: NORDATLANTEX '96
3-stamp souvenir sheet
Children's drawing

Fiji

1973: Development Projects
10 Cents
Small bicycle

Finland

1942: Hame Bridge
50 Markka
Small bicycle

1979: Centenary Business and Industry Regulation
1.10 Markka

1989: Sports
1.90 Markka

France

1960: Museum of Art & Industry
30 Francs

1974: 47th Congress of Federation of French Philatelic Societies
50 Centimes
Small bicycle

1978: Sports for All
1 Franc

1986: 50th Anniversary Popular Front
2.20 Francs

1991: PHILEXJEUNES '91
2.50 Franc

1995: Winter Velodrome Raid
2.80 Francs
No bicycle on stamp, "Rafle du Vel d'Hiv"
(Raid at the Winter Velodrome)

French Polynesia

1960: Post Office, Papeete
16 Francs

1989: Tahiti Post Office
40 Francs
Small bicycle

1989: Copra Industry
70 Francs
Small bicycle

1992: Centenary of first stamp
200 Francs
Small bicycle

1993: J. Boulaire Paintings
32 Franc
Pahi Morrea

39 Francs
Pahi Rurutu

51 Franc
Pahi Nuku-Hiva

French West Africa

1958: Centenary of Dakar
25 Francs
Small bicycle

Gambïa

1990: Stamp World London '90
8 Dalasy
Mickey Mouse

1990: Industry
5 Bututs
10 Bututs

1993: Centennial of Ford Engine
2 Dalasy
Also appears on 12-stamp souvenir sheet

1995: ECOWAS
2 Dalasy
Small bicycle

German Democratic Republic

1953: Stalin Allee
24 Pfennig
Small bicycle – 2 varieties exist
Also issued twice with 20 Pfennig overprint

1955: Stalin Allee
20 Pfennig
Issued in 2 varieties

1955: German Buildings
15 Pfennig
Small bicycle

1959: Stalin Allee
20 Pfennig
Small bicycle

1966: Traffic Safety
25 Pfennig

1968: Fighters of the Underground
10 Pfennig
Small bicycle in stained glass window

1976: Dogs
5 Pfennig
Bicycle shadow

1978: Circus
10 Pfennig
Elephant on a tricycle

1985: Circus
35 Pfennig
Jugglers on unicycles

Germany

1991: Traffic safety
100 Pfennig

1994: Re-opening of Berlin Wall
100 Pfennig
Bicycle wheel

Ghana

1967: 50th Anniversary of Ghana Boy Scouts
3-stamp souvenir sheet
Bicycle in selvedge

12-stamp souvenir sheet
All 4 New Pesewas
Bicycle in selvedge
Also issued in souvenir sheets of twelve 10 New
Pesewas and twelve 12 ½ New Pesewas stamps

1971: 2nd Ghana International Trade Fair
20 New Pesewas

1991: 17th World Jamboree
100 New Cedi
Stamp on stamp

600 New Cedi
Stamp on stamp

1-stamp souvenir sheet – 800 New Cedi
Stamp on stamp
Above stamps and souvenir sheet also each issued
with overprints

Gibraltar

1995: Centenary of Cinema
4-stamp souvenir sheet
Bicycle on tab only

Grenada

1992: Thrill Sports
1 Dollar
Donald Duck on mountain bike

Grenada Grenadines

1989: PHILEXFRANCE '89
10 Cents
Mickey & Minnie Mouse on tandem

1991: Save Our Planet
5 Dollars
Scrooge McDuck using pedal power

Guatemala

1953: National Fair
65 Centavos

Guernsey

1982: Cobo Bay
20 Pence

1985: St. Saviours Church
8 Pence

1991: King's Mill, St. Saviours
21 Pence

1992: Historic Trams
28 Pence
Small bicycle

1994: Christmas
24 Pence
Tricycle
Also appears on 6-stamp souvenir sheet

Guinea

1963: Sports
1.50 Franc
10 Francs
200 Francs

Guyana

1984: President's 60th Anniversary
25 Cent over 1.30 Dollar
No bicycle, stamp overprinted "Cycling"

1.20 Dollar over 1.30 Dollar
No bicycle, stamp overprinted "Cycling"

1990: Locomotives
1-stamp souvenir sheet – 20 Dollars
Bicycle in selvedge

1992: Toy Trains
9-stamp souvenir sheet
Bicycle in selvedge
Iissued in series of 8 – 8th sheet has bicycle on
center stamp

1992: Toy Trains
1-stamp souvenir sheet – 350 Dollars
Bicycle in selvedge
Issued in series of 8

1992: World Thematic Exhibition
600 Dollars
Issued in both gold and silver foil stamps
Both gold and sliver stamps appear on
1-stamp sheets
Both gold and silver stamps appear together on
1-stamp sheet
Both gold and silver stamps each appear on
1-stamp "125th Anniversary of Baseball" sheets

1993: Christmas
600 Dollars
Tricycle
Issued in both silver and gold foil
Each stamp appears on 3 souvenir sheets: two
1-stamp, 4-stamp

1995: Disney Characters at Work
35 Dollars
Mickey Mouse as a paper boy
Also appears on 6-stamp souvenir sheet

1996: Supersports
9-stamp sheet
Donald Duck on BMX bike

Haiti

1953: Special Delivery
25 Centimes
Small bicycle

Hong Kong

1985: Historic Buildings
5 Dollars
Small bicycle

Hungary

1953: Sports
20 Filler
Opening of the People's Stadium, Budapest

1965: Circus
4 Forint
Bear on bicycle

1973: Light Your Bicycle
1 Forint

1973: Skylab
1-stamp souvenir sheet
10 Forint
Exercise bicycle in selvedge

1976: 30th Anniversary Hungarian Pioneers
1 Forint

Iceland

1986: Centennial of National Bank
13 Krona
Small bicycle

1990: Post Offices
21 Krona
Small bicycle

Ifni

1958: Sports
70 Centimos

1964: Stamp Day
50 Centimos
1.50 Peseta

India

1954: Centenary of India's Postage Stamps
4 Annas

1991: International Conference on Traffic Safety
6.50 Rupee

Indonesia

1977: 9th National Sports Week
50 Rupiah
Bicycle symbol only

1992: Hari Anak National
75 Rupiah

1996: Scouting Jamboree
1.50 Rupiah
Scout on unicycle
Also appears on 1-stamp souvenir sheet –
1250 Rupiah

Iran

1985: International Youth Year
5 Rials
Bicycle symbol only

Ireland

**1981: Youth Hostel Association
50th Anniversary**
15 Pence

1992: Health
28 Pence

1995: Narrow gauge railways
52 Pence
Also appears on 4-stamp souvenir sheet
(also issued with "Singapore '95" logo)

Isle of Man

1991: Ramsey Harbor Tramway
17 Pence

1992: World War II
28 Pence
Soldier on bicycle
Also appears on 8-stamp souvenir sheet

1994: Tourism
24 Pence

1995: Steam-Powered Vehicles
24 Pence

Israel

1966: Traffic Safety
5 Agorot

1994: Health
85 Agorot
Bicycle on tab only

1996: Sports
1.05 Shekel

Italy

1954: 60th Anniversary Italian Touring Club
25 Lira

1964: Stamp Day
15 Lira
Stamp on stamp

1968: Stamp Day
25 Lira
Bcycle symbol only

1980: Stamp Day
70 Lira

1983: Stamp Day
300 Lira
Spaceman with bicycle

1988: Italian Films & Directors
650 Lira
The Bicycle Thief movie

1994: Italian Touring Club Centennial
600 Lira

Italy – Trieste

1951: 60th Annivers. Touring Club of Italy
25 Lira
"AMG-FTT" overprinted on 1954 Italy stamp

1954: 1951 World Cycling Championships
25 Lira
"AMG-FTT" overprinted on 1951 Italy stamp

Ivory Coast

1969: PHILEXAFRIQUE
100 Francs
Painting by Achalme

1971: 11th Anniversary of Independence
35 Francs
Small bicycle

1974: Stamp Day
35 Francs
Small bicycle

1984: Stamp Day
100 Francs
Small bicycle

1984: 90th Anniversary Ivory Coast Postage Stamps
125 Francs
Stamp on stamp
Small bicycle

Japan

1958: Shimonoseki-Moji Tunnel
10 yen
Small bicycle

1990: International Garden and Greenery Exposition
62 Yen
Small bicycle

Jersey

1990: Post Offices
18 Pence
Small bicycle

Jordan

1970: Sports
100 Fils

1977: Postal Savings Bank
10 Fils

Kenya Uganda Tanzania

1974: 10th Anniversary of Zanzibar Revolution
70 Cents
Small bicycle

Kiribati

1988: Australian Assistance Causeway Construction
15 Cents

Korea, North

1965: Anniversary Rubber Workers Strike
10 Chun

1972: Chollima Street
5 Chun
Small bicycle

1972: President's Anniversary
40 Chun

1976: Health
40 Chun

1980: Day of the Child
10 Chun
Tricycle
Also appears on 6-stamp souvenir sheet

1987: Traffic Signs
10 Chun
Bicycle symbol only

1994: Circus
40 Chun
Jugglers on unicycles
Also appears on 4-stamp souvenir sheet

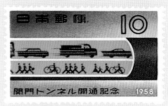

Kuwait

1966 World Health Day
8 Fils
Small bicycle

10 Fils
Small bicycle

Laos

1973: 25th Anniversary Laotian Scout Movement
125 Kip

1974: Transportation
90 Kip
Pedi-cab
Also appears on 4-stamp sheet

1979: Asian-Oceanic Postal Union
5 Kip
100 Kip

1988: 125th Anniversary International Red Cross
52 Kip
Hand-pedaled three-wheeler

Lesotho

1983: Manned Flight Bicentenary
60 Sente
Small bicycle

Liberia

1957: Founding of Antoinette Tubman Child Welfare Foundation
4 Cents
Tricycle

1994: Train Paintings
1-stamp souvenir sheet
1 Dollar
Small bicycle

Libya

1981: International Year of the Child
20 Dirhams
Small bicycle

Liechtenstein

1958: Sports
90 Rappen

1985: 40th Anniversary of the Red Cross
50 Rappen

Luxembourg

1970: Traffic safety
3 Francs
Small bicycle

1994: World War II
14 Francs
Small bicycle

Macao

1987: Traditional Transportation
10 Patacas
Trishaw

1988: Transportation
20 Avos

1995: Senado Square
2 Patacas
Small bicycle
Also appears on 16-stamp sheet

1996: Communications
1-stamp souvenir sheet – 8 Patacas
Trishaws in selvedge

Madagascar

1956: FIDES Economic and Social Development Fund
3 Francs
Small bicycle

Malaysia

1994: 100th Anniversary of Electric Supply
30 Cents

1996: International Day Against Drug Abuse
30 Cents

Maldive Islands

1992: EuroDisney
1-stamp souvenir sheet – 20 Rafiyaa

Malta

1996: 50th Anniversary UNICEF
25 Cents
Tricycle

Marshall Islands

1989: PHILEXFRANCE '89
1-stamp souvenir sheet – 1 Dollar

Mexico

1975: Exporta
1.60 Peso
4 varieties produced

1987: Exporta
20 Peso

1988: Paintings by Antonio Ruiz
300 Pesos
"Parade"

1991: Exporta
2100 Peso
Also issued without cross-hatching

Monaco

1974: International Circus Festival
1.10 Francs

1984: Paintings by Hubert Clerissi
4 Francs
Small bicycle

1990: Automobile Club Centennial
4 Francs

Mongolia

1973: Circus Scenes
5 Mung
Chimpanzee on a bicycle

15 Mung
Bear on a unicycle

1974: Mongolian Circus
80 Mung
Unicyclist

Namibia

1992: Tourism
25 Cents
Small bicycle
Also appears on 4-stamp souvenir sheet

Netherlands

1983: Royal Dutch Touring Club Centenary
70 Cents
Bicycle sign

1988: Modern Transportation Meeting Ecological Requirements
75 Cents
55 Cents

1990: Post Offices
55 Cents
Small bicycle

75 Cents
Small bicycle

1993: 100th Anniversary Bicycle-Automobile Industry
70 Cents
80 Cents
No bicycle on stamp, "Rijwiel" (bicycle) printed on stamp

1994: 100th Anniversary Dutch Motoring Association
70 Cents
Bicycle symbol only

1996: Vacations
80 Cents

Nevis

1982: 75th Anniversary of Scouting
5 Cents

New Zealand

1985: Early Transportation
58 Cents

Nicaragua

1949: 10th World Series of Amateur Baseball
5 Centavos
40 Centavos
Both stamps also appear on 4-stamp sheet

1977: 75th Anniversary of Graf Zeppelin
5 Centavos
Small bicycle

Nigeria

1972: Introduction of Right-Hand Driving
4 Pounds

Niuafo'ou

1990: 150 Years of Stamps
2.50 Pa'anga
Stamp on stamp
Also appears on 20-stamp sheet

1996: 50th Aniversary of UNICEF
80 seniti
Tricycle
80 seniti
Children on bicycles

Niue

1974: Christmas
3 Cents

1975: Children's Drawings
5 Cents

Norway

1979: Boat on Skjernoysund
1.25 Krone
Small bicycle

Palau

1987: Japanese Links to Palau
44 Cents

1991: Tourism and Industry
30 Cents
Also appears on 16-stamp sheet

Panama

1986: Christmas
36 Centavos
Tricycle under green tree

42 Centavos
Tricycle under silver tree

Papua New Guinea

1983: World Communications Year
10 Toea

1986: Lutheran Church Centennial
70 Toea
Small bicycle

1992: Japanese Nankai Force
60 Toea

1996: Centenary of Radio
1 Kina

Paraguay

1977: Aviation History
2 Guarani
Small bicycle

1985: Great Week of Aviation Painting
1-stamp souvenir sheet – 25 Guarani

1989: 40th Anniversary Federal Republic of Germany
Label – velodrome on label
Also appears on 5-stamp, 4-label sheet

Philippines

1979: 1st Scout Philatelic Exhibition
5-stamp souvenir sheet
1959 Semi-Postal souvenir sheet overprinted
and revalued

Portugal

1978: Sport for all People
10 Escudo

1992: Machine-vended labels
Around 24 values with toy high-wheeler

Portuguese India

1961: Sport
4 Escudo

Redonda

1983: Balloon Anniversary
1-stamp souvenir sheet – 5 Dollars
Bicycle in selvedge

Romania

1969: Circus Performers
10 Bani
Juggler on a unicycle

1972: Romanian Aviation Pioneers
3 Lei

1987: Traffic Safety
50 Bani

1994: Circus
150 Lei
Monkeys on unicycles

Russia

1949: Sports
40 Kopecks

1954: Sports
40 Kopecks

1958: Russian Cities
40 Kopecks
Lenin statue, Tashkent
Small bicycle

40 Kopecks
University Square, Frunz
Small bicycle

1959: Russian Writers
40 Kopecks
Small rear half of bicycle

1967: 50th Anniversary of October Revolution
4 Kopecks
"Farmers Holiday" painting by S.V. Gerasimov

1980: 20th Anniversary Gagarin Cosmonaut Training Center
32 Kopecks
Exercise bicycle

1980: Intercosmos Cooperative Space Program (USSR–Cuba)
15 Kopecks
Exercise bicycle

1980: Intercosmos Cooperative Space Program (USSR–Hungary)
6 Kopecks
Exercise bicycle

1987: Intercosmos Cooperative Space Program (USSR–Syria)
5 Kopecks
Exercise bicycle

1988: Animated Soviet Cartoons
5 Kopecks

Rwanda

1985: Self-Sufficiency in Food Production
10 Francs

1985: International Youth Year
9 Francs

Saint Kitts

1985: Batik Art
60 Cents

1987: Sugar Cane Industry
75 Cents

Saint Lucia

1981: 100th Anniversary of Picasso
1-stamp souvenir sheet

5 Dollars
"Night Fishing at Antibes"

1985: International Youth Year
45 Cents
Tricycle

Saint Thomas & Prince Islands

1982: 75th Anniversary Scouting
15 Dobra
Stamp on stamp
Also appears on 6 souvenir sheets:
three 2-stamp, three 8-stamp

1983: Braziliana "83
6-stamp souvenir sheet – flying bicycle
in selvedge

Saint Vincent

1964: Boy Scout 50th Anniversary
1 Cent – Bicycle merit badge
4 Cents – Bicycle merit badge
20 Cents – Bicycle merit badge
50 Cents – Bicycle merit badge

1991: Flintstones Enjoy Sports
5 Dollars

1994: Hong Kong '94 Stamp Exposition
40 Cents
Stamp on stamp
Also appears on 10-stamp sheet

1996: Disney Occupations
50 Cents
Goofy as a bicycle messenger
Also appears on 9-stamp souvenir sheet

Saint Vincent Grenadines

**1989: India '89 International
Stamp Exhibition**
25 Cents
Goofy driving pedicab

1991: 90th Birthday Queen Elizabeth
1-stamp souvenir sheet – 5 Dollars
Small bicycle at Royal Lodge, Windsor
in selvedge

1-stamp souvenir sheet – 5 Dollars
Small bicycle, Buckingham Palace in selvedge

1994: Hong Kong '94 Stamp Exposition
40 Cents
Stamp on stamp
Also appears on 10-stamp sheet

Salvador, El

1992: Ecology
60 Centavos
5 Colon

San Marino

**1994: 100th Anniversary Italian
Touring Club**
1000 Lira

**1995: Qianmen Complex of
Zhengyangmen Rostrum**
1500 Lira
Small bicycle

Sharjah

1972: Sports
1 Rupee
Also appears on 6-stamp souvenir sheet

Sierra Leone

1990: Christmas
50 Leone
Also appears on 8-stamp souvenir sheet

1993: Christmas
1200 Leone
Tricycle in selvedge

1995: Disney Circus
200 Leone
Clarabelle Cow on unicycle

1995: Disney Christmas
1000 Leone
Toy Goofy on a bicycle

1996: Centenary of Cinema
250 Leone
Small bicycle
Also appears on 9-stamp sheet

Singapore

1971: Tourism
15 Cents
Trishaw

30 Cents
Trishaw

1987: River Life
1 Dollar

1989: Old Chinatown
10 Cents
Painting of Sago Street

35 Cents
Painting of Pagoda Street

1990: Tourism
30 Cents
Trishaw in front of Raffles Hotel

1992: Machine-vended labels
Various values
Trishaws

1995: Meet in Singapore
2-stamp souvenir sheet
Stamp on stamp, bicycle in selvedge

1996: Native Trees
No denominations, "For local addresses only"
Small bicycles

Solomon Islands

1996: Transportation
90 Cents

Somalia

1958: Sports
1.20 Somali

South Africa

1986: Johannesburg Centenary
14 Cents
Small bicycle

1994: Children's Art
45 Cents

South Africa – Bophuthatswana

1978: Road safety
10 Cents
20 Cents

1982: 75th Anniversary of Boy Scouts
15 Cents

1985: Specialized Bicycle Factory
8 Cents

South Africa – Ciskei

1986: Bicycle Factory in Dimbaza
14 Cents
20 Cents
25 Cents
30 Cents

South Africa – Transkei

1983: Post Offices
20 Cents

Spain

1960: Sports
40 Centimos
2 Peseta

1979: Health
8 Peseta

1983: ports
13 Peseta

Sri Lanka

**1990: 175th Anniversary Sri Lanka
Postal Service**
10 Rupee

Surinam

1945: Bauxite Mine, Moengo
1 Cent
Small bicycle

**1967: 10th Anniversary Central Bank
of Surinam**
10 Cents
Small bicycle

25 Cent
Small bicycle

1968: 100th Anniversary C. Kersten & Co.
30 Cents
Small bicycle

**1979: International Year of the Child
30th Anniversary SOS Children's Villages**
20 Cents
Small bicycle

Sweden

1977: Physical Fitness
95 Ore

1983: Nordic Cooperation Issue
1.65 Krona

1986: Christmas
1.90 Krona

1987: Bicentennial Circus in Sweden
2.10 Krona
Unicyclist on tightrope

1987: Illustrations from Children's Novels by Astrid Lindgren
1.90 Krona

1989: Summer
2.10 Krona

1990: Post Offices
2.50 Krona
3.80 Krona
Small bicycle

1995: Tourism
5 Krona

1996: Summer Scenes
3.85 Krona
Painting by Sven X. Erixson

1996
3.85 Krona
Delivery cycle

Switzerland

1983: Bicycle and Motorcycle Federation Centenary
70 Centimes

Tanzania

1990: Cog Railroads
8 Shillings

1992: Literacy Year
35 Shillings
Scrooge McDuck on a unicycle
Also issued on 9-stamp souvenir sheet

1992: Pope
100 Shillings
Also appears on 12-stamp sheet

1994: World War II
200 Shillings
Also appears on 6-stamp souvenir sheet

Togo

1978: 75th Anniversary of Motorized Flight
200 Francs
Also appears on 2-stamp souvenir sheet

1990: Stamp Day
90 Francs

1995: History of Transportation
200 Francs
Also appears on 9-stamp souvenir sheet

Tonga

1991: Accident Prevention
42 Seniti
Also issued with Tongan text
Both stamps also on 20-stamp sheet
Both stamps also issued revalued at 60 Seniti
Re-valued stamps also appear on 20-stamp sheet

1993: Health and Fitness
2.50 Pa'anga

Also appears on 10-stamp sheet

1993: Family Planning
45 Seniti
Also issued with Tongan text
Both stamps also appear on 20-stamp sheet

1993: 75th Birthday King Taufa'ahau Tupou IV
80 Seniti
Also appears on 9-stamp sheet

1995: 25th Anniversary Children of the Commonwealth
45 Seniti
Also issued with "Singapore "95" logo

60 Seniti
Also issued with "Singapore "95" logo

80 Seniti
2 Pa'anga
2.50 Pa'anga

1995: Singapore '95 World Stamp Exhibition
1-stamp souvenir sheet – 2 Pa'anga

1996: 50th Aniversary of UNICEF
80 Seniti
Tricycle

80 Seniti
Children on bicycles

Turkish Republic of Northern Cyprus

1986: Painting
100 Turkish Lira
"Ataturk Square" by Yalkin Mahtaroglu

1990: Post Offices
1500 Turkish Lira
Small bicycle
Also appears on 4-stamp sheet

Tuvalu

1988: 125th Anniversary International Red Cross
1-stamp souvenir sheet – 1.50 Dollar
Bicycle in selvedge

Uganda

1987: Transportation Innovations
2 Shillings
Pedal-powered airplane

1988: Disney Christmas
50 Shillings
Also appears on 8-stamp souvenir sheet

1990: World Health Organizations
600 Shillings
Mickey Mouse

1992: Goofy about Stamps
100 Shillings

1994: Automotive Anniversaries
700 Shillings
Small bicycle

Umm Al Qiwain
1974: Sport
1 Riyals
3-D stamp

United Arab Emirates
1993: National Youth Festival
50 Fils

United Nations – Geneva
1987: United Nations Day
12-stamp sheet, all 50 Centimes
No bicycle stamp, bicycle on sheet margins

12-stamp sheet – all 35 Centimes
No bicycle stamp, bicycle on sheet margins

United Nations – New York
1987: United Nations Day
12-stamp sheet – all 22 Cents
No bicycle stamp, bicycle on sheet margins

12-stamp sheet – all 39 Cents
No bicycle stamp, bicycle on sheet margins

1988: Health in Sports
25 Cents

1995: International Youth Year
55 Cents

United Nations – Vienna
1987: United Nations Day
12-stamp sheet – all 5 Schillings
No bicycle stamp, bicycle on sheet margins

12-stamp sheet – all 6 Schillings
No bicycle stamp, bicycle on sheet margins

United States
1970: Christmas Toys
6 Cents
Tricycle

1987: 75th Anniversary Girl Scouts
22 Cents
Cycling merit badge

Uruguay
1927 Philatelic Exposition
2 Centesimos – small bicycle
5 Centesimos – small bicycle
8 Centesimos – small bicycle
Each stamp appears on separate 4-stamp sheet

1979: Rowland Hill Centennial
2-stamp souvenir sheet
Stamp on stamp
Small bicycle

1996: Transportation
3.20 Peso

Vietnam
1984: 30th Anniversary Dien Bien Phu
1 Dong

1987: Reconstruction Progress
5 Dong

1988: Tourism
40 Dong

1989: Hoi Cong Da 1789-1989
100 Dong

1995: Traditional Women's Attire
400 Dong

Yemen Arab Republic
1970: PHYLIMPIA London 1970
1-stamp souvenir sheet – 4 Bogaches
Stamp on stamp, bicycle in selvedge

1980: World Scouting Jamboree
60 Fils
Also appears on 1-stamp and 6-stamp
souvenir sheets

Yemen, Peoples Democratic Republic
1972: Arab Youth Week
10 Fils

Yugoslavia
1985: Children's Drawings
70 Dinar

1995: Peace & Freedom
1.90 Dinar
Tricycle
Also appears on 8-stamp sheet

Yugoslavia – Trieste
1952: Sport
5 Dinar

Zanzibar and Tanzania
1966: Karibuni Visiwani
50 Cents
Small bicycle

10 Shillings
Small bicycle

Zimbabwe
1990: Transportation
33 Cents
35 Cents
Bicycles on top of bus

8

Local Issues

Mail throughout the world has not always been delivered by employees of governmental postal authorities. Sometimes private ventures have sprouted up — erratically and mostly short-lived — to seize the opportunity to supply a usually secluded area with private mail service. The stamps produced are called "local" issues, and many times don't show up on topical checklists. For the cycling philatelist, local issues can be fun but usually difficult to collect. Many of the issues are almost a century old, and most were issued in small quantities.

Coolgardie

One of the first local issues with cycling interest was the brainchild of James A. Healy, an Australian businessman in the late 1800s. Gold discovered in the Coolgardie district of Western Australia in 1892 swelled the population of the colony from 58,000 to 161,000 in five years, and Healy saw an opportunity to make money by operating a private mail delivery service between the goldmines. Using bicycles, and later camels, the messengers of Healy's "Coolgardie Cycle Express Company" provided daily service to the goldfields. (The government only delivered mail weekly.) The initial route covered the 120 miles between Coolgardie and Southern Cross, a

Shown here is a reproduction of a postcard issued by the Coolgardie Cycle Express Co. in 1894 advertising their new cycle express service which subsequently was suppressed by the Western Australian Post Office.

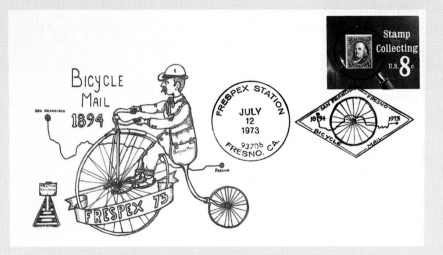

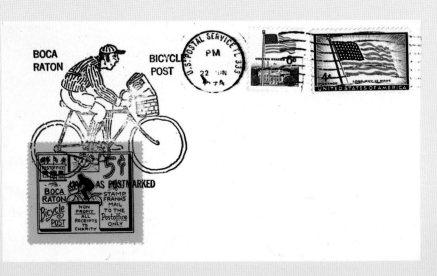

10-hour one-way trip by bicycle. Soon, though, the service reached all the way to Lake Darlot, 280 miles north of Coolgardie.

In 1894, Healy produced two stamps in two different denominations, each carrying an illustration of a bicycle and the name of the company. A year later, when camels were put into operation, three additional stamps were issued, still carrying the "Coolgardie Cycle Express Company" verbiage but showing camels instead of bicycles. The camel stamps were short-lived, however. Two days after the stamps went on sale, the Western Australia Government shut down Healy's private mail operation. During the three-year venture, his couriers pedaled more than 260,000 miles.

While numerous bicycle mail services operated in the Coolgardie area at the same time, only two issued postage stamps: Healy's company, and another whose stamps pictured a red (or pink) swan and included the words "Cycle Mail." (In 1986, a pair of Cycle Mail stamps sold for $5,000 Australian.)

Fresno–San Francisco

Around the same time as the Coolgardie, local bicycle services were in operation, a similar bicycle post made a brief run in the United States. When an American Union Railway strike brought mail delivery to a halt between Fresno and San Francisco (and much of the nation), cyclist Arthur Banta decided to implement a private mail-carrying service using bicycles as transport.

The service began on 7 July 1894 and used eight relays to cover the 210 miles between the two cities. One delivery along the entire route took about 18 hours. A Fresno engraver and stamp collector named Eugene Donze designed and printed a diamond-shaped stamp for the mail service. While Donze could engrave he couldn't spell, at least not "San Francisco." After printing a first set of stamps with the city's name misspelled, he corrected the die and printed a new batch.

Banta's private mail delivery service cost 25 cents plus the usual 2 cents charged by the U.S. Postal Service. Three days after the railway strike settled on 15 July, the bicycle mail delivery service terminated.

Cape of Good Hope–Mafeking

One of the most famous private mail bicycle delivery services also spurned the creation of the Boy Scouts. In 1900, during the Boer war in southern Africa, Colonel Robert Baden-Powell of the British Army commanded a force of 1,000 soldiers to defend the town of Mafeking in the Cape of Good Hope. For 217 days Powell's forces thwarted the loosely organized armies of Boers (farmers whose Dutch ancestors had started settling the land in 1652). During the siege, Powell organized a group of cadets, nicknamed "Boy Scouts" to deliver messages through enemy lines. The price of capture for the scouts by the Boers was death; the reward for getting through, first a cow, and later £25, a lot of money at the turn of the century.

Baden-Powell organized another corps of cadets to deliver mail within the besieged city. Stamps produced to offset the cost of the service included a 3 penny issue which carried an illustration of Baden-Powell and a 1 penny denomination showing Sergeant Major Warner Goodyear, one of Baden-Powell's energetic underlings, on a bicycle. The stamps saw service from April 9 to when the siege ended on May 17.

When Baden-Powell returned to England amidst a hero's welcome, he discovered boys using training exercises from a manual he had written for his soldiers: "Aids to Scouting." He eventually rewrote the manual into a 182-page book called "Scouting for Boys" and organized the first Boy Scouting outing, a 2-week camp for 22 teenage youngsters.

Couriers for Upper Italy

When World War II knocked out communications in upper Italy in February 1945, a company named Corrieri Alta Italia, or Coralit, received authorization from the Ital-

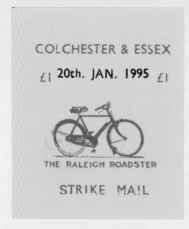

ian government to provide bicycle mail service between major cities in northern Italy. Coralit's service was pricy, but considering the bicycle couriers reduced the time it took to get a letter from, say, Turin to Trieste, from the normal three weeks to four or five days, most customers found the service worth it.

On average, cyclists rode up to 60 miles a day, with one day off for each two days worked. The couriers were paid 75 lire per day, plus 2.5 lire per kilometer ridden, and 30 lire for meals. The cyclists only delivered mail between cities — from post office to post office — not locally.

Of the stamps issued for the service, seven carried bicycle designs: two showed a bicycle wheel on a map of northern Italy, the other five a cyclist on the same map.

Other Notable Local Issues

A loophole in German postal regulations in 1886 saw as many as 160 towns set up private mail services. Bicycles were used to transport the mail, as were balloons, even carrier pigeons. Of the cities that used bicycles, Hamburg, Bochum, and Frankfurt produced stamps carrying an image of a bike. The German government halted all private mail delivery services in 1900.

The Barcelona Postal Express appears to be the longest running private bicycle mail service, operating from 1904 to 1933 in Spain, and issuing the greatest number of local bicycle stamps — 210.

In England, the Colchester Scouts have been operating an annual non-profit operation since 1989, delivering mail by bicycle throughout Colchester Borough, but only during Christmastime. New bicycle stamps are issued by the scouts every year.

Other private bicycle mail services that have issued bicycle stamps have been operated in other parts of England (even one operation that delivered mail only by high-wheel bicycle), as well as the Netherlands, New Zealand, and Boca Raton, Florida.

9

Booklets

Luxembourg produced the first "official" stamp booklet, in 1895, although private booklets were introduced in the United States eight years earlier. The stamp booklet offers the opportunity for advertising on all covers, both inside and out, and on the interleaves and possible labels inside. Germany was the first to exploit advertising in their booklets, in 1910, and other countries were soon to follow. Everything from Mohawk tires to Copenhagen coal and coke have been pitched by postage stamp booklets.

For the bicycle philatelist, booklets have been issued containing cycling stamps inside, and/or bicycle illustrations on the covers. However, only five booklets (excluding private issues) have had both: cycling stamps and cover illustrations as part of the same booklet.

The first, produced by Norway in 1979, shows a bicycle so small it's hardly worth mentioning. The booklet cover and stamp carry the same photo of a boat and buildings along the shore of Skjernoysund. A bicycle leans against one of the buildings.

The second combo booklet was issued by Australia as part of the country's 1989–90 "Sporting Activities" stamp series. Sue Passmore — one of the artists highlighted in Chapter 11 — designed the stamps and booklet. A black-and-white drawing of the lower half of a road bicycle stretches across the entire front and back booklet cover, along with a full-color reduced reproduction of the cycling stamp. Inside are ten 41-cent stamps.

In 1993, Monaco produced a booklet carrying a front-cover illustration of a bicycle racer, gleaned from a portion of the bicycle stamp inside. The cover art shows just the bike's handlebars, top of the front wheel, and gloved hands grasping the drops of the bars, along with glimpses of two other sports: downhill skiing and archery. Inside the booklet are six stamps, all 2.80 franc denomination, depicting bobsledding, skiing, sailing, rowing, swimming, and cycling. Another booklet holding six 4.50-franc stamps, none of which show a bike, used the same cover.

The most recent booklets carrying bicycle art on the cover and on a stamp inside come from Sweden and Singapore, and were both issued in 1996. The Swedish stamps commemorate "Summer in Art" and were produced from famous Swedish paintings. The bicycle issue reproduces a painting by Sven X. Erixson (1899–1970) with a portion of the picture (showing a girl on a one-speed bicycle) also used for the booklet cover.

The Singapore issue commemorates Native Trees and shows three cyclists (two on a tandem) pedaling underneath a Kayu Manis tree. Hongkong Bank sponsored the stamp issue as part of their "Care for Nature" environment conservation and education program, launched in 1989.

Great Britain produced two booklets carrying bicycle art on the cover. The first, issued in February, 1972 (and again in April), shows a British Pillar Box and a postman holding onto an 1860s-period bicycle. Inside the booklet are stamps, of course, but also advertisements for the "Sun Life of Canada Retirement Plan."

Great Britain also produced a series of six "Costume" booklets in 1982. The cover of the sixth in the series shows women in 1880s-period attire, two of them holding bikes.

Thailand issued a series of 25 booklets from 1 January 1990 through the end of 1991. The cover of all the booklets carry the same illustration: a postman pedaling a bicycle. The stamps inside the booklets commemorate everything from Songkran Day

$4.10
10 x 41c STAMPS

41c

AUSTRALIA

Australia Post

10ᴾ

Stamps
2 each at
½p, 1p
1½p, 2p

1 kg

Sommar
i konsten

Valör 3:85 Pris 38:50

1880-1900
Sixth of six
illustrations by
Eric Stemp on
nineteenth century
women's costume.
Printed by
Harrison &
Sons Limited.

(Year of the Sheep) to the International Productivity Congress.

In 1990, the Isle of Man produced a booklet commemorating "Railways & Tramways." The cover shows three cyclists pedaling past a working train.

Denmark issued a couple of booklets with bicycle representation. The first shows a cyclist pedaling past a church, the other, produced in 1995, celebrates the 50th anniversary of the European liberation by Allied forces. Other bicycle booklets come from Ireland and Belgium.

Two Irish issues — in 1987 and 1989 — contain reproduced bicycle stamps (from earlier series) on the back covers. A Belgian booklet of 1984 carries an illustration on the inside cover of a postman pedaling a bicycle while transporting a package perched on the palm of his hand.

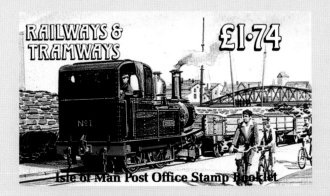

10

Other Postal Items

In this chapter, we'll discuss the other items of interest to philatelists: First Day Covers, Maximum Cards, and Postal Stationery.

First Day Covers

First day covers, or FDCs, are envelopes bearing a stamp and postmark commemorating the first day a particular stamp was issued. Many FDCs also contain an illustration (called a cache) that ties into the stamp. First day covers are produced by postal administrations, philatelic companies (Artmaster, Fleetwood, and Colorano, for example in the U.S.), and individuals. Many commercially-produced FDCs may also contain information pertaining to the subject being commemorated on the stamp on the reverse side of the envelope.

Literally hundreds of first day covers contain cycling interest either by stamp, cache or both. Many times the same stamp can be found on numerous FDCs, each illustrated with a different cache, and released by competing first day cover issuing companies. For instance, the 50th Giro d'Italia, in 1967, saw first day covers issued in at least three different cities: Rome, Milan and Florence, by three first day cover producing companies.

One Rome cover carries a cache of a miniaturized version of the poster issued for the first Giro, in 1909. The poster (and cache) is printed in pink, replicating the color of the pages of *La Gazzetta dello Sport*, the sports daily that organized the race (the Giro's leader's jersey is pink as well). Another cache features a map of Italy showing each of the Giro's stages in the 1967 race, while another carries an illustration of 3 cyclists superimposed across the front page of *La Gazzetta dello Sport*.

First day covers often contain a cycling cache but not a cycling stamp. A cover produced for the U.S. Olympic Committee, for instance, shows a cancel, not for the first day issue of the stamp (a 6 cent "flag" stamp) affixed to the envelope, but for the first day of the Olympic Cycling Trials competition, on 22 August 1968 at the Encino Velodrome in Southern California. First day covers may also contain a cycling stamp, but no cycling cache (or no cache at all), like the 1996 Aruba FDC commemorating the 1996 Olympic Games. The first day cover is affixed with the two-stamp Olympic set canceled in Aruba on 28 May and is imprinted with a cache of the 1996 Atlanta Olympic logo.

Another type of FDC is the hand-painted first day cover. Like rare art, some hand-painted FDCs are signed and numbered, and most are produced in small quantities. Because of their unique design and limited release, hand-painted FDCs are usually priced higher than mass-produced first day covers. One such FDC, by an independent artist, contained the following mimeographed message inside the envelope:

As you can see, this cover bears an "unofficial" first day cancellation. My friends Allison Cusick and Tom Lane purchased the stamps in Wheeling, West Virginia, and drove to Dayton, Ohio for the Wright Bros. Branch post office cancellation. For the caper I designed this cache — I had used a similar drawing on a Wright Brothers cover in 1978.

T. Michael Weddle

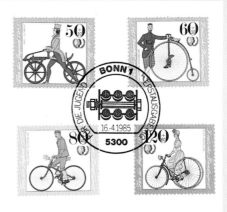

Bicycling in Germany
Popular since the early 1800s,
bicycling is an integral part of life in Germany.

F.D.C. "ROMA"

LE VÉLOCIPÈDE

Many first day covers also carry "fancy cancels." In addition to the date and place of cancellation, a fancy cancel will also include an illustration that ties in with the stamp or event being commemorated by the first day cover. An example is a 1962 World Cycling Championships FDC, issued in Belgium, which includes a postmark replicating one of the stamps in the 2-stamp set. Another example is a French FDC released in 1983. The stamp and cache commemorate Pierre and Ernest Michaux's contribution to bicycle design: the postmark carries an illustration of Michaux's velocipede.

Maximum Cards

Buy a stamp and a postcard with the same or similar subject of the stamp, affix the stamp to the picture side of the card, and voila, you have produced a Maximum Card.

Maximum cards have been around since the late 1800s, becoming popular from 1930 to 1945. They are still in demand today, so much so that maximum card collecting has its own philatelic name: Maximaphily.

Maximum cards are produced by postal administrations, philatelic companies (generally with the approval of postal administrations), and individuals. Many maximum cards contain a "First Day of Issue" cancellation.

An example of a maximum card issued by a philatelic company is from the Dutch firm Zegelkoerier. Using a copy of a 1980 Netherlands semi-postal stamp commemorating the 75th Anniversary of the Netherlands' National Preservation Society, the company produced a postcard based on an enlargement of the stamp. The stamp was then affixed to the card and canceled by the post office. Included on the back side of the postcard is information about the stamp:

theme, designer, size, perforation, and so on.

An individually produced maximum card example is a postcard from the Ohio Historical Center in Columbus, Ohio. An individual purchased the card, affixed three United States 5.9-cent bicycle stamps, then had the stamps cancelled at the first day of issue city for the stamps, Wheeling, West Virginia.

Postal Stationery

Postal cards, envelopes with postal stamps embossed or imprinted, and aerograms comprise postal stationery.

For the bicycle philatelic collector, Russia is the king in postal stationery, having issued approximately 65 cards, envelopes and aerograms carrying the image of a bicycle. Russian postal stationery has commemorated numerous cycling competitions including the Spartakiad Games, Peace Races, and bicycle racing in the 1980 Moscow Olympics. Also, Russian postal stationery promotes traffic safety (showing a cyclist traveling in the wrong direction on a roadway), the circus (a performer on a unicycle), and a youth sports hall.

Postal stationery showing a bicycle has also been issued by the U.S. Postal Service, most recently for the 1996 Olympics, in sets of 20 postal cards each depicting a different Olympic sport.

Mexico has produced bicycle postal stationery (an envelope embossed with the $1.60 "Exporta" stamp), Sweden with an aerogram, Australia, to commemorate the 175th anniversary of postal service in Australia, Poland for the Warsaw–Berlin–Prague bicycle races, Great Britain with four postal cards on the history of cycling, and South Korea with a set of postal cards commemorating the 1988 Seoul Olympics.

11

The Artists

Without artists, postage stamp art would not exist. Here is a look at four artists who have designed bicycle stamps.

Professor Paul Flora, Austria

Clowns sporting long, fake red noses on Ordinary bicycles; barrel-chested, overweight, mustached men racing in a velodrome — the bicycle stamp designs of Austria's Professor Paul Flora are easy to spot.

Born in 1922 in Glurns, South Tyrol (the very northern part of Italy that once belonged to Austria), Professor Flora has drawn and painted for as long as he can remember.

After moving to Innsbruck with his family as a kid, he enrolled at the Munich Academy in 1942, mostly to avoid military service. However, two years later he found himself carrying a gun instead of a paintbrush, anyway. "I only fired one shot during the war," Flora said. "I had to stand sentry, and I heard a strange noise. I asked for the password ... another strange noise ... so I shot. It turned out to be a cow. We had good food for a while."

After the war his first art exhibition took place in Berne, Switzerland, in 1945. Since then Professor Flora (the "Professor" moniker is an honorarium) has published 40 books on his art, exhibited all over the

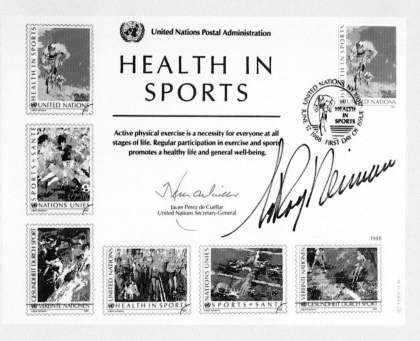

world, and for 15 years supplied more than 3,000 political caricatures to *Die Zeit*, a German weekly newspaper published in Hamburg. His drawings have also appeared in numerous newspapers around the globe including the *New York Times*.

"I worked as a caricaturist because I had the ability, but I always regarded myself as an artist. At any rate, I didn't mind what I drew as long as it showed quality."

Of his two bicycle stamp designs, the first came in 1985, on commission from Austria Post.

The Austrians are very interested in art, and they commission an artist every year to

SPORT SERIES – II

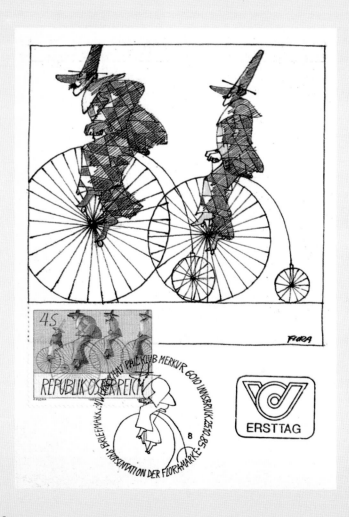

do something special. Every artist does something typical of himself. He called his design of the clowns on bikes "just fantasy."

His next bicycle stamp commission came in 1988 from Liechtenstein, a country for which he has done numerous designs. The 4-stamp set entitled "1988 Summer Olympics, Seoul – Sports Pioneers" again shows his whimsical sense of style. In addition to the aforementioned velodrome racers, the set includes stamps that portray barrel-chested runners, gymnasts, and equestrians.

Other Liechtenstein stamps illustrated by Professor Flora include a 4-stamp set for the 1988 Winter Olympics, three stamps for the 15th Anniversary of the Kirchplatz Theater, and a design commemorating the 500th Anniversary of European Postal Communications. And for 1998, Professor Flora has been commissioned to produce another Liechtenstein stamp, on the subject of letters: "Love letter, something you get from court, someone wanting money from you, any kind of letter," he says.

His philosophy of life is simple: "Not too much work, read a lot, walk a lot, travel a lot." It corresponds well with his art philosophy: "You should draw what gives you pleasure, and don't take on too many commissions."

LeRoy Neiman, United States

LeRoy Neiman has painted just about every sport imaginable, from soccer to chess, and from basketball to horse racing. He has been commissioned to paint many of the world's most famous sporting events including the Super Bowl, Indianapolis 500, Kentucky Derby, and the Masters Golf Tournament.

Mr. Neiman, who lives in New York City, has illustrated for *Playboy* magazine (every issue for 42 years, and counting), painted live on television, and has produced 11 books. His art has been exhibited all over the world.

Born in 1927 in St. Paul, Minnesota, Mr. Neiman started drawing at an early age, knowing that creating art would be his life.

"I used to do my own comic strip. Most kids that are good, that have national talent, will draw comics as a starter. [Back then] I didn't think about drawing sports stuff very much. I drew what I was around. When I was a kid, sports weren't as big as they are now. There was no television."

After serving in the army for four years during World War II, Neiman enrolled at the prestigious School of the Art Institute of Chicago. Upon graduation he taught figure and fashion drawing at the school for ten years. When the United Nations contacted him in 1988 to use six of his paintings as illustrations for a set of "Health and Welfare" stamps, Neiman already reigned as one of the pre-eminent sports artist in the world. His "Bikes and Boats I," painted in 1973, became the subject for one of the stamps in the United Nations set.

"I used to go to France every summer and knock around in the Riviera and they [bicycle racers in the Tour de France] were coming through the mountains." The painting shows the eventual winner of the race, Luis Ocana of Spain, in the leader's yellow jersey, struggling up a steep pitch.

"My earliest memory of bicycle racing was Reggie McNamara, a six-day bike racing champion when I was a kid, in the '30s. He was a hero. Reggie McNamara was right up there with Babe Ruth and Jack Demsey and those kind of people in that great period of early sports." (McNamara participated in 117 6-day races from 1913 to 1936.) "I've got drawings from bicycle racing at the Olympics, the Tour DuPont. It's a great sport, and it's very visual."

LeRoy Neiman has painted some of the world's greatest bicycle racers, including Jacques Anquetil, Bernard Hinault, and Greg LeMond.

In 1994, Neiman was again contacted by the United Nations, this time to produce original art for a 1996 6-stamp "Sport and the Environment" set. The stamps would contain both the 1996 Olympic Games logo and Olympic rings. Using acrylics, he executed three paintings, two sports illustrated on each: cycling and track & field, volleyball and basketball, and hurdling and gymnastics.

"I wanted to do boxing (Mr. Neiman's favorite sport to paint), but they didn't want to do that."

He says the inspiration for the bicycle stamp came from watching racing at the Moscow Velodrome.

"I have a style, I know that. I have a style that is recognized. My style is the result of an accumulation of all the artists I have looked at going way back to the Renaissance and through the years. A little bit rubs off, and then, for no particular reason, something happens.

"I know that I'm living today, and so I paint what I experience today. I'm not reflective or futuristic. I'm not a ground breaker. I just respond to my own experiences wherever I am."

Sue Passmore, Australia

Artist Sue Passmore of Melbourne, Australia, remembers her first pedal-powered vehicle: "A tricycle, fixed wheels with a tray on the back. Very cool!" About the same time as she received her tricycle she took up drawing.

"I loved drawing as a kid, and it grew from there, I guess." She eventually earned a diploma in graphic design, worked for Australia Post and in studios around Melbourne, before opening a studio with her husband, Jim, in their home. She specializes in graphic design, illustration, and packaging and publication design. From 1983 to the present, Passmore has the distinction of designing more Australian stamps than any other artist. In 1989 she received a commission from the Australia Post Philatelic Research Group to produce art for a series of definitive stamps on a variety of sporting activities, including bicycling.

With her cycling design, Passmore says she tried to convey "a sense of cycling as a fun activity which can be enjoyed by anyone with a bike." She says a definite directive from the design brief stated all riders on the stamp must wear a helmet. The brief also called for her to produce art for the ancillary products, as well — first day covers, and booklet.

While she has no favorite subject to draw — "I'll have a go at just about anything" — she does favor working with colored pencils, acrylic gouache, and watercolors. Her professional goals are to "Improve with every illustration I attempt." When she's not working, Passmore enjoys aerobics, gardening, movies and cycling. "My husband and I both ride lightweight, 12-speed racers."

Gyula Vasarhelyi, England

Nobody in the world has produced more postage stamp art than England's Gyula Vasarhelyi. He is cited in the *Guinness Book of Records, Facts and Feats* as the world's most prolific stamp designer.

Since his first stamp design (a 1962 Surinam floral issue), Vasarhelyi has produced over 6,000 stamps and First Day Covers for 148 countries. That 67-year old Vasarhelyi works 14–16 hours every day of the year, and has no outside interests, is of no surprise.

"I don't have time for hobbies," he says, "but whilst I am working, I like to listen to classical music, mainly opera."

Already a student of art for 10 years, in 1956, Vasarhelyi fled his native Hungary the day the Secret Police came searching for him to inquire about his revolutionary activities. After fleeing his homeland, he continued his studies in London at the Royal Academy of Art, and on scholarship in India, Indonesia, and Peru. In 1965, he finally settled in Darlington, England, where he taught art at the College of Technology while working part-time on stamp design. Years later, he resigned from the college to concentrate full-time on stamp art.

"I always have commissions coming to me from all parts of the world. I have just completed, for the Northern Cook Islands, Penrhyn and Aitutaki, an Olympic issue, and also an issue to commemorate HM Queen Elizabeth II 70th birthday. At the moment, I am planning out designs for Christmas 1996."

While he has drawn everything — from Santa Claus playing golf (for a Christmas Island stamp set), to astronauts landing on the moon, to Shakespearean plays, to birds and turtles — his favorite subjects are portraits and figure compositions. And his favorite medium is oil. But in the business of stamp design, he says, he's forced to use gouache which works better when preparing the art for printing.

Vasarhelyi's stamps have become so popular that some people collect only his designs — more than likely because of his attention to detail. He paints the stamp art four times the projected size, fattening spokes on a bicycle wheel or wrinkles on faces to ensure they will show when the art is reduced. His 1992 "Railways of the World" stamps for Grenada, for instance, each took over 40 hours to draw, not including research time.

"I was the first stamp designer to design stamps in eight colors, to the horror of the agent who was handling it. He thought the designs would not sell; in fact they went into reprint twice over."

Bicycles have been included on two of Vasarhelyi's designs, both for the 1992 Olympics, for the Cook Islands and Cayman Islands. The Cook Islands triptych is tied together with a wave-like border running through the three stamps to show continuity. And to "give the impression of speed" in the Cayman Island set, Vasarhelyi chose to show only a portion of the bicycle and rider in three of the four stamps. The set received the "Stamp of the Month" award by the Crown Agents Stamp Bureau, a London company that designs and produces stamps for numerous postal authorities all over the world.

So while Vasarhelyi continues to listen to his classical and opera music as he paints, he sees no end to his philatelic masterpieces. "I am a commercial artist, and I have to do what the client commissions. I can only make sure that each piece of work is as attractive as possible."

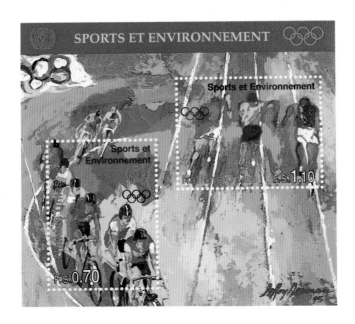

12

Errors on Stamps

Like life, stamp design isn't perfect. Sometimes errors are made. The Cuba Special Delivery stamp of 1899 contained an error in spelling: "Immediata" instead of "Inmediata." While the mistake was discovered almost immediately, the U.S. Post Office, who supplied the stamps, decided to wait until the initial stock of stamps had been depleted before producing a new plate and printing corrected stamps. Another mistake in spelling on a bicycle stamp occurred almost 100 years later. The African nation of Gambia issued an 8-stamp souvenir sheet in 1995 commemorating past Summer Olympians. Nelson Vails, Match Sprint silver medalist at the 1984 Los Angeles Games, is identified on a 3-Dalasy denomination stamp as Nelson "Valis."

Greg LeMond might not be too happy with a Tanzania 1990 stamp release. The 30 Shilling stamp identifies Ronan Pensec as the 1990 Tour de France winner. LeMond won the race not only in 1990, but in 1986 and 1989 as well. Pensec has never finished first.

Staying in Africa, Bophuthatswana issued a 4-stamp set promoting road safety. "Stop signs are there for your safety," the stamp picturing a bicycle states. But how's the guy supposed to stop? His bike has no brakes.

Track bicycles on the road and road bikes on the track appear to be a problem with stamp designers.

Portuguese India produced a 1961 stamp showing a cyclist riding a brakeless bike on a sandy road.

A 1992 Olympic stamp from Gabon portrays two racers duking it out on what appears to be a wooden track — only they're on road bikes.

In 1984, St. Vincent produced a 2-stamp set entitled "Leaders of the World." One stamp shows a track rider racing the velodrome, the other a racer on a brakeless, gearless bicycle competing on pavement.

A 1984 Trinidad and Tobago stamp has the track rider on the right bike and on a velodrome, but he's going the wrong way.

Bermuda, for the 1996 Olympics, issued a 30-cent stamp showing three cyclists in a sprint for the finish. However, each of their bikes are equipped with aero bars — which are not used in a road race.

And the U.S. produced a sheet of 20 Olympic stamps, one showing a bicycle, for the 1996 Atlanta Games. While the verbiage on the reverse describes sprint racing, the stamp shows a pursuit bike.

A few stamp designers decided to fudge on the location of the chain and derailleurs. On a Cayman Islands 1993 "Tourism" stamp, a 1991 Aland stamp, and a 1996 Guyana Disney stamp, the artist chose to locate the chain on the left side of the bike instead of the right, as is customary.

Then there's a Yemen Arab Republic 1981 souvenir sheet, on which the artist left off the entire rear half of the bicycle.

13

Getting Started

Getting started in bicycle stamp collecting is as easy as cycling to your local post office and checking out the new issues. Do any of them contain a bicycle? If the answer is yes, buy them, and you're on your way.

Next, explore your phone book for stamp stores in your area. Many dealers have display binders filled with sets of topical stamps to peruse. Joining the "Bicycle Stamps Club" is also highly recommended. The club's quarterly newsletter will keep you informed on world-wide bicycle stamps (and other bicycle philatelic material) just released, plus interesting background information on bicycle stamps. You'll also be able to swap and buy stamps from fellow members.

When you're ready to get serious about bicycle stamp collecting, you'll need to develop a "Want List" of stamps and corresponding catalogue numbers. The world's four major catalogue companies are Scott, in the United States, Germany's Michel, Yvert et Tellier in France, and Great Britain's Stanley Gibbons.

Each uses its own unique numbering system. It will take some time, but for your Want List, you'll need to copy down each corresponding catalogue number for each bicycle stamp. (You can buy current stamp catalogues from the catalogue companies themselves, from stamp dealers, or through ads in philatelic publications, or you can browse through a set for free at your local library.)

With your Want List, re-visit your local stamp dealer. Depending on what part of the world you live in, you can call up the Scott, Michel, Yvert, or Stanley Gibbons numbers from your list, and the dealer will check to see if he has them in stock.

In addition, you can purchase bicycle stamps at stamp shows and bourses in your area. Many philatelic publications print a calendar listing such events. Stamps can also be purchased through the mail — again check out the stamp publications for company advertisements. The Internet is also a good source for the stamp collector. The two best links are:

"Joseph Luft's Philatelic Resources on the Web" at http://www.execpc.com/~joeluft/resource.html

and

"Chuck Hendricksen's Philatelic Links Page" at http://www.netxpress.com/users/winphins/philhp.html.

You may also wish to sign up for a New Issues Service. Every month you will receive an accumulation of bicycle stamps (or practically any other topic) that have been recently issued from the service. You can find a New Issues Service through advertisements in philatelic catalogues and publications.

If you're on a budget, collect used stamps; they're usually less expensive than mint stamps.

Most stamps come in sets. And most dealers won't break a set to sell you an individual stamp. However, while at a stamp show seek out the "country" dealers first. Many times they'll sell you individual stamps.

Pertinent Contacts

Bicycle Stamps Club

Tony Teideman
P.O. Box 90
Baulkham Hills, NSW 2153
Australia

or

Bill Hofmann
610 N. Pin Oak Lane
Muncie, IN 47304
U.S.A.

or

Tore Josefsson
Ostra Gunnesgarde 8c
S-41743 Goteborg
Sweden

Catalogue Companies

Scott Publishing Company
911 Vandemark Rd..
Sidney, OH 45365
U.S.A.

Stanley Gibbons Publications Ltd
5 Parkside
Chirstchurch Rd.
Ringwood, Hampshire BH24 3SH
Great Britain

Michel, Schwaneberger Verlag GmbH
Muthmannstrasse 4
D-80939 Munchen 45
Germany

Yvert et Tellier
37 rue des Jacobins
80036 Amiens
France

New Issues Services

Bombay, Inc.
P.O. Box 7719
Delray Beach, FL 33484
U.S.A.

M&N Haworth
P.O. Box 20
Clitheroe, Lancs. BB7 2JQ
Great Britain

Max Stern & Co.
234 Flinders St.
Melbourne, Victoria 3000
Australia

Herman Sieger
Venusberg 32–34,
3545 Lorch
Germany

Theodore Champion, S.A.
Paris Montholon B.P. 3
Paris, Cedex 75430
France

Glossary

Approvals
Stamps sent from a dealer to you "on approval," meaning you're under no obligation to buy.

Block
At least four unseparated stamps (two up and two down).

Booklet Pane
Stamps in a booklet.

Bourse
A marketplace for stamps.

Cachet
A design on an envelope. Used for first day covers, philatelic exhibitions, and so on.

Cancellation
Mark to show that a stamp has been used.

Coils
Stamps in a roll.

Commemoratives
Stamps that honor people or events.

Definitives
Regular stamps, usually used over a long period of time, like flag stamps in the United States.

Face Value
The monetary value of a stamp.

Imperforate
Stamps issued without perforations.

Label
Usually attached to a stamp, but carrying no postage value.

Mint
A stamp that has never been used.

Overprint
Additional printing on a stamp that wasn't part of the original design.

Pane
A full sheet of stamps.

Postmark
Shows date and location of post office where letter or parcel was mailed.

Selvedge or selvage
Border on souvenir sheet.

Souvenir Sheet
Colorful adhesive sheet usually commemorating an event or anniversary, and usually containing one or more postage stamps within its borders.

Surcharge
On a semi-postal stamp, the amount paid in addition to postage. The surcharge is usually collected for a cause or organization.

Bibliography

"Australian Record." *Stamp Magazine*, February 1986.

Batho, Norman. "List of Bicycle Stamps." 1994.

Batho, Norman. "Checklist of Bicycle Related Postal Stationery from Russia." *Bicycle Stamps*, Winter 1993–4.

Baur, Brian C. "Semi-postals popular idea, but nixed in U.S." *Stamp Collector*, 16 July 1994.

Bicycle Stamps, Spring, 1993 through Summer 1996.

Cabeen, Richard McP. *Standard Handbook of Stamp Collecting*, New Revised Edition. New York: Thomas Y. Crowell, Publishers, 1979.

Carey, Alan. "Prolific Perfectionist – Gyula Vasarhelyi, stamp designer." *Gibbons Stamp Monthly*, July 1987.

Caribbean Commonwealth: Front Matter, *Countries of the World*, 01-01-1991.

Enhagen, Carl-Olaf. *Sports Stamps*. New York, New York: Arco Publishing Company, Inc., 1961.

Filanci, Franco. "But Where Do You Go to be a Postman on a Bike?" *Cronaca Filatelica*, February 1980.

Fitzpatrick, Jim. *The Bicycle and the Bush: Man and Machine in Rural Australia*. Oxford University Press, 1980.

Furman, Vsevolod. "A Splendid Issue for An Aborted Spartakiade." *Journal of Sports Philately*, Issue 1, 1992.

Gray, Ian. "The 'Centre Cycle.' " *Stamps*, September 1982.

Griffenhagen, George and Jerome Husak. *Adventures in Topical Stamp Collecting*. Milwaukee: American Topical Association, 1981.

Henry, Bill. *An Approved History of the Olympic Games*. Los Angeles: The Southern California Committee for the Olympic Games, 1981. "History of the Ancient Olympics." Australian Sports Commission.

"History of the Modern Olympics." Australian Sports Commission.

Hueseler, Rob. "Accused duPont heir owns stamp rarity." *Linn's Stamp News*, February 12, 1996.

Ilma, Viola. *Funk & Wagnalls Guide to the World of Stamp Collecting*. New York: Thomas Y. Crowell, Publishers, 1978.

John Player & Sons. *Cycling cigarette cards*. 1939.

Jones, Margaret. "Sport Stamps: Behind the Scenes, Part 3." *Journal of Sports Philately*, Issue 1, 1978.

Kandaouroff, Prince Dimitry. *Postmarks, Cards and Covers: Collecting Postal History*. New York: Lorousse and Co., Inc., 1973.

Krause, Barry. "Collecting Boer War Mail." *Antiques & Collecting Magazine*, May 1996.

Lacko, Joseph. "Prague–Berlin–Warsaw Bicycle Races." *Journal of Sports Philately*, Issue 9–10, 1969.

Malone, Steve. *Illustrated Bikes on Stamps*. Shoreline, Washington, 1996.

Marchant, Douglas. "Netherlands Dutch Reward Cards 'For the Child.' " *Bicycle Stamps*, Autumn 1989.

Marchant, Douglas. "The Prague Scout Local 'Cycle' Post of 1918." *Cycle Slips*.

Martin, M. W. *Topical Stamp Collecting*. New York, New York: Arco Publishing Company, Inc., 1975.

Moore, Barbara and Honor Holland. *The Art of Postage Stamps*. New York: Walker and Company, 1979.

O'Keefe, Donna. "Bicycle mail service created scarce covers." *Linn's Stamp News*, March 31, 1986.

"Olympic Tradition." Australian Sports Commission.

Perrault, Gilles. *The Red Orchestra*. New York: Simon and Schuster, 1969.

Perry, David B. *Bike Cult*. New York: Four Walls Eight Windows, 1995.

Peterson, Robert. "The Fathers of Scouting." *Boys' Life*, September 1994.

Pridmore, Jay and Jim Hurd. *The American Bicycle*. Osceola, Wisconsin: Motorbooks International, 1995.

"Putting a Stamp on the World." *The Daily Telegraph*, February 26, 1988.

Ritchie, Andrew. *King of the Road, An Illustrated History of Cycling*. Berkeley, California: Ten Speed Press, 1975.

"Sri Lankan Postmen Threatening Strike." *Bicycle Retailer and Industry News*, May 1, 1996.

Teideman, Tony. "Fabulous Four Depicted on Stamp." *Australian Bicycle*. October 1986.

United States Cycling Federation, *U.S. Cycling Team Media Guide*. Colorado Springs: United States Cycling Federation, 1994.

Waltl, Rupert and Steve Malone. "Albert Richter." *Bicycle Stamps*, Winter 1996.

Watson, James. *The Stanley Gibbons Book of Stamps and Stamp Collecting*. New York: Crescent Books.

Wedd, Monty. "The Coolgardie Cycle Express Co." *Linn's Stamp News*, November 12, 1984.

Wedgwood, Barry. "Gyula L Vasarhelyi, Creator of Masterpieces in Miniature." *Gibbons Stamp Monthly*, August, 1994.

Wiedman, Carl. "Local Heroes – The Delivery of Private Mail by Cyclists." *Bicycle Stamps*, Spring, 1993.

Williams, L. N. "Rare local franked mail during gold rush." *Linn's Stamp News*, February 10, 1986.

Index

A

addresses (of resources) 140
animated characters, 91
approvals, 141
art, 89–90
artists (stamp designers),
   131–137
Asian semi-postals, 73

B

Bibliography, 142–143
Bicycle Stamp Club, 140
block, 141
booklet pane, 141
booklets, 12, 123–130
bourse, 141
Boy Scouts, 82

C

cachet, 141
cancellation, 141
Cape of Good
   Hope–Mafeking,   121
catalogue companies, 140
Cinderellas, 13
coil, 141
commemorative stamps, 10,
   141
Coolgardie, 119
Couriers for Upper Italy, 121

D

definitive, 141
Draisienne, 14
Du Pont, see Triathlon

E

errors, on stamps, 10, 138
European semi-postal stamps,
   71–73

F

face value, 141
fancy cancel, 12

first bicycle stamp
first day covers, 12, 126
Flora, Paul, 131
Fresno–San Francisco, 121

G

Giro d' Italia, 53
Glossary, 141

H

health and safety, 90–91
Hill, Rowland, 9
history 9–11, 14–20
   of bicycle 14–17
   of stamps,9–10

I

imperforate, 141
Internet (as resource), 139
IOC (International Olympic
   Committee), 21
   centennial, 25

L

label, 141
LeRoy Neiman, 135
local issues, 13, 119–122

M

maximum cards, 12, 129
Merckx, Eddy, 55
mint, 141
mistakes, see errors
modern bicycle, 17

N

new issue services, 139–141

O

Olympics, 21–51
Olympic mascot, 23
Ordinary bicycle, 15
overprint, 73, 141

P

pane, 141
Passmore, Sue, 136
Peace Race, 53–54
philately, 12–13, 139–141
Philatelic Link Page, 139
Philatelic Resources on the
   Web, 139
postal bikes, 80
postal carriers, 11, 80–88
postal stationery, 12, 129–130
postmark, 141

R

Racing, 52–70
   see also Olympics
resources, 139"140

S

safety, see health and safety
safety bicycle, 16
selvedge (or salvage), 141
semi-postals, 12, 71–79
souvenir sheet, 12, 141
stamp collecting, 13, 139–141
stamp designers, see artists
surcharge, 141

T

track racing, 24, 54
transportation, 90
triathlon, 55
Tour de France, 53

U

Upper Italy, see Couriers for
   Upper Italy

V

Vasarhelyi, Gyula, 136

W

women postal carriers, 81